MW01248755

The Harcourt Brace Casebook Series in Literature

"A & P"

John Updike

THE HARCOURT BRACE CASEBOOK SERIES IN LITERATURE
Series Editors: Laurie G. Kirszner and Stephen R. Mandell

DRAMA
Athol Fugard
"Master Harold" . . . *and the boys*

William Shakespeare
Hamlet

POETRY
Emily Dickinson
A Collection of Poems

Langston Hughes
A Collection of Poems

SHORT STORIES
Charlotte Perkins Gilman
"The Yellow Wallpaper"

John Updike
"A & P"

Eudora Welty
"A Worn Path"

The Harcourt Brace Casebook Series in Literature
Series Editors: Laurie G. Kirszner and Stephen R. Mandell

"A & P"

John Updike

Contributing Editor
Wendy Perkins
Prince George's Community College

Harcourt Brace College Publishers

Fort Worth   Philadelphia   San Diego   New York   Orlando   Austin   San Antonio
Toronto   Montreal   London   Sydney   Tokyo

Publisher:	Earl McPeek
Executive Editor:	Michael Rosenberg
Acquisitions Editor:	Julie McBurney
Developmental Editors:	Laura Newhouse/Katie Frushour
Project Editor:	Andrea Wright
Art Director:	Vicki Whistler
Production Managers:	Linda McMillan/James McDonald

ISBN: 0-15-505484-8
Library of Congress Catalog Card Number: 98-70269

Copyright © 1998 by Harcourt Brace & Company

All rights reserved. No part of this publication may be reproduced or transmitted in any form or by any means, electronic or mechanical, including photocopy, recording, or any information storage and retrieval system, without permission in writing from the publisher.

Requests for permission to make copies of any part of the work should be mailed to: Permissions Department, Harcourt Brace & Company, 6277 Sea Harbor Drive, Orlando, Florida 32887-6777.

Copyright acknowledgments begin on page 109 and constitute a continuation of the copyright page.

Harcourt Brace College Publishers may provide complimentary instructional aids and supplements or supplement packages to those adopters qualified under our adoption policy. Please contact your sales representative for more information. If as an adopter or potential user you receive supplements you do not need, please return them to your sales representative or send them to: Attn: Returns Department, Troy Warehouse 465 South Lincoln Drive, Troy, MO 63379.

Address for orders:
Harcourt Brace & Company
6277 Sea Harbor Drive, Orlando, FL 32887-6777
1-800-782-4479

Address for editorial correspondence:
Harcourt Brace College Publishers
301 Commerce Street, Suite 3700, Fort Worth, TX 76102

Web site address:
http://www.hbcollege.com

Printed in the United States of America

8 9 0 1 2 3 4 5 6 7   066   9 8 7 6 5 4 3 2 1

ABOUT THE SERIES

The Harcourt Brace Casebook Series in Literature has its origins in our anthology *Literature: Reading, Reacting, Writing* (Third Edition, 1997), which in turn arose out of our many years of teaching college writing and literature courses. The primary purpose of each Casebook in the series is to offer students a convenient, self-contained reference tool that they can use to complete a research project for an introductory literature course.

In choosing subjects for the Casebooks, we draw on our own experience in the classroom, selecting works of poetry, fiction, and drama that students like to read, discuss, and write about and that teachers like to teach. Unlike other collections of literary criticism aimed at student audiences, The Harcourt Brace Casebook Series in Literature features short stories, groups of poems, or plays (rather than longer works, such as novels) because these are the genres most often taught in college-level Introduction to Literature courses. In selecting particular authors and titles, we focus on those most popular with students and those most accessible to them.

To facilitate student research—and to facilitate instructor supervision of that research—each Casebook contains all the resources students need to produce a documented research paper on a particular work of literature. Every Casebook in the series includes the following elements:

- A comprehensive **introduction** to the work, providing social, historical, and political background. This introduction helps students to understand the work and the author in the context of a particular time and place. In particular, the introduction enables students to appreciate customs, situations, and events that may have contributed to the author's choice of subject matter, emphasis, or style.

- A **headnote,** including birth and death dates of the author; details of the work's first publication and its subsequent publication history, if relevant; details about the author's life; a summary of the author's career; and a list of key published works, with dates of publication.

- The most widely accepted version of the **literary work,** along with the explanatory footnotes students will need to understand unfamiliar terms and concepts or references to people, places, or events.

- **Discussion questions** focusing on themes developed in the work. These questions, designed to stimulate critical thinking and discussion, can also serve as springboards for research projects.

- Several extended **research assignments** related to the literary work. Students may use these assignments exactly as they appear in the Casebook, or students or instructors may modify the assignments to suit their own needs or research interests.

- A diverse collection of traditional and non-traditional **secondary sources,** which may include scholarly articles, reviews, interviews, memoirs, newspaper articles, historical documents, and so on. This resource offers students access to sources they might not turn to on their own—for example, a popular song that inspired a short story, a story that was the original version of a play, a legal document that sheds light on a work's theme, or two different biographies of an author—thus encouraging students to look beyond the obvious or the familiar as they search for ideas. Students may use only these sources, or they may supplement them with sources listed in the Casebook's bibliography (see below).

- An annotated model **student research paper** drawing on several of the Casebook's secondary sources. This paper uses MLA parenthetical documentation and includes a Works Cited list conforming to MLA style.

- A comprehensive **bibliography** of print and electronic sources related to the work. This bibliography offers students an opportunity to move beyond the sources in the Casebook to other sources related to a particular research topic.

- A concise **guide to MLA documentation,** including information on what kinds of information require documentation (and what kinds do not); a full explanation of how to construct parenthetical references and how to place them in a paper; sample parenthetical reference formats for various kinds of sources used in papers about literature; a complete explanation of how to assemble a List of Works Cited, accompanied by sample works cited entries (including formats for documenting electronic sources); and guidelines for using explanatory notes (with examples).

By collecting all this essential information in one convenient place, each volume in The Harcourt Brace Casebook Series in Literature responds to the needs of both students and teachers. For students, the Casebooks offer convenience, referentiality, and portability that make the process of doing research easier. Thus, the Casebooks recognize what students already know: that Introduction to Literature is not their only class and that the literature research paper is not their only assignment. For instructors, the Casebooks offer a rare combination of flexibility and control in the classroom. For example, teachers may choose to assign one Casebook or more than one; thus, they have the option of having all students in a class write about the same work or having different groups of students, or individual students, write about different works. In addition, instructors may ask students to use only the secondary sources collected in the Casebook, thereby controlling students' use of (and acknowledgment of) sources more closely, or they may encourage students to seek both print and electronic sources beyond those included in the Casebook. By building convenience, structure, and flexibility into each volume, we have designed The Harcourt Brace Casebook Series in Literature to suit a wide variety of teaching styles and research interests. The Casebooks have made the research paper an easier project for us and a less stressful one for our students; we hope they will do the same for you.

Laurie G. Kirszner
Stephen R. Mandell
Series Editors

PREFACE

John Updike's "A & P" was first published in *The New Yorker* in 1961, a year that saw the inauguration of John Fitzgerald Kennedy, who heralded an age of significant change for all Americans. The previous decade had set the stage for the major political and social transformations that would soon be realized in the 1960s.

"A & P" reflects the social and personal realities of this era through the story of Sammy, a nineteen-year-old supermarket checkout clerk faced with a decision that could have a major impact on his future. Updike paints a sympathetic portrait of this teenager, who is caught between his need for individuality and his sense of duty. Sammy's conflicting urges and his subsequent actions produce a coming-of-age story that is as relevant today as it was in 1961.

The sources in this casebook present a wide variety of perspectives. Some analyze elements of "A & P," while others explore the body of Updike's work; some provide biographical details, while others comment on historical, social, psychological, and aesthetic aspects of "A & P" or of Updike's work in general. Together with the study questions and research assignments, these sources will help you gain insight into the story and then develop your own critical interpretation of it.

- Updike, John. "Still Afraid of Being Caught." Updike takes a look back at his childhood, especially at incidents when he was caught, or almost caught, for "doing something wrong." He also generalizes about the reasons why children commit acts that society considers "transgressions."

- Mizener, Arthur. "Behind the Dazzle Is a Knowing Eye." In this review of Updike's *Pigeon Feathers and Other Stories,* the collection of short stories that includes "A & P," Mizener presents both positive and negative criticism of Updike's verbal style in his previous work. Mizener then claims that in this collection of stories, Updike successfully combines verbal "dazzle" with deep insight into the human condition.

- Luscher, Robert M. "Ceremonies of Farewell: *Pigeon Feathers.*" *John Updike: A Study of the Short Fiction.* Luscher examines the themes and narrative techniques of "A & P" and "Lifeguard."
- Murray, Donald. *Interview with John Updike.* In this interview with critic and poet Donald Murray, Updike provides viewers with a unique insight into what prompted him to write "A & P" and analyzes Sammy's character and motivation as well as the consequences of his actions.
- Murray, Donald. E-mail to Tim Westmoreland. In this E-mail message Murray comments on his own adolescent experiences as well as on the social and economic implications of "A & P."
- Murray, Donald. "Amid Onions and Oranges, a Boy Becomes a Man." In this newspaper column, Murray focuses on Sammy's coming of age in "A & P" and reflects on his own memories of growing up in a small town.
- Updike, John. "Lifeguard." This story, published with "A & P" in a collection of Updike's short stories titled *Pigeon Feathers and Other Stories* (1962), is an expanded version of the original ending of "A & P." Following the suggestion of his editor at *The New Yorker,* Updike cut the original last few pages of "A & P," which told of Sammy going to the beach in vain to look for the girls.
- Wells, Walter. "John Updike's 'A & P': A Return Visit to Araby." This article compares "A & P" to James Joyce's "Araby," arguing that both stories focus on a "poor romantically infatuated young boy" who finds "a reality that frustrates him." Walter's analysis points out similarities in the characters' psychology as well as differences between the stories' settings that affect the characters' behavior.
- Dessner, Lawrence Jay. "Irony and Innocence in John Updike's 'A & P.'" This essay focuses on the story's structure and its ironic ending.
- McFarland, Ronald E. "Updike and the Critics: Reflections on 'A & P.'" McFarland's article presents a critical overview of Updike's work in general and "A & P" in particular. After summarizing both positive and negative views of "A & P," McFarland offers his own interpretation of how Updike uses symbolism in the story to comment on contemporary American society.
- Porter, M. Gilbert. "John Updike's 'A & P': The Establishment and an Emersonian Cashier." This critical article proposes that Sammy acts as an Emersonian hero, especially when he asserts his individuality.
- Steiner, George. "Supreme Fiction: America Is in the Details." Steiner

discusses lost values in the face of American materialism, a theme that pervades much of Updike's work.

In addition to these sources, the Casebook also includes a student paper illustrating MLA documentation style and format. Student author Tim Westmoreland uses several of these sources, including a videocassette of an interview with Updike, showing how print and nonprint sources can be effectively integrated into an essay. Tim's main focus is on Sammy's feelings of social inequality and his attempt to cross class lines. Tim presents his interpretation of how Sammy's feelings motivate his decision to quit his job. Notice that the author does not allow the sources to dominate his paper. His own voice remains distinct throughout as his ideas are supported by his research.

Acknowledgments

No project as ambitious as the Casebook series happens without the help of many talented and dedicated people. First, I would like to thank everyone who was involved with the first and subsequent editions of *Literature: Reading, Reacting, Writing,* particularly Laurie Kirszner and Stephen Mandell. Next, I would like to thank the people who worked with me on the "A & P" Casebook: acquisitions editor Julie McBurney, developmental editor Laura Newhouse, production managers Linda McMillan and James McDonald, art director Vicki Whistler, and project editor Andrea Wright. Finally, I would like to thank Michael Rosenberg, who suggested the idea of a Casebook series, and without whose enthusiastic help and support this series would never have come into being.

CONTENTS

Sample Student Research Paper 71

An annotated essay in which student Tim Westmoreland examines the theme of social inequality in "A & P."

Bibliography 81

A bibliography of print and electronic sources, including a list of Updike's works, biographical profiles of and interviews with the author, criticism and commentary on his works, and resources for understanding America in the 1950s and early 1960s.

Introduction

America's "New Frontier"

In his acceptance speech at the 1960 Democratic National Convention, John F. Kennedy announced, "We stand today on the edge of a new frontier—the frontier of the 1960s—a frontier of unknown opportunities and perils—the frontier of unfulfilled hopes and threats." America stood on the brink of change at the beginning of the 1960s, at the onset of a decade of sweeping political, technological, cultural, and social transformations. The previous decade in America had heralded these changes and set the stage for the "opportunities and perils" and the "hopes and threats" that would shortly be realized in the 1960s. John Updike's short story "A & P," published in 1961, straddles these two decades, anticipating the voices of change to be heard in the 1960s as well as echoing those voices that still asserted the status quo of the 1950s.

"THE AFFLUENT SOCIETY"

In *The Affluent Society,* published in 1958, John Kenneth Galbraith examined American consumerism in the 1950s, a time when more than ever before, Americans had the money not only to acquire necessities, but also to spend on "conveniences" and "improvements" to their lives. The higher standard of living enjoyed by Americans during this period was a direct result of the United States's participation in World War II, which enabled the country to become the strongest and most prosperous economic power in the world. The money that poured into defense spending helped to create a successful military-industrial complex that bolstered the economy: companies produced goods that enabled them to become prosperous and hire more workers, who could in turn buy more goods.

In this "age of plenty" customers could choose from a wide variety of innovations; the two most popular were new automobiles and suburban homes, both of which became important status symbols. Car manufacturers sold 21 million new cars during this period, most with powerful V-8 engines, tail fins, and lots of chrome. Developer William J. Levitt dotted the American suburban landscape with developments that crammed together hundreds of inexpensive, assembly-line houses with wall-to-wall carpeting and fully mechanized kitchens. Americans' exodus to the affordable housing of the suburbs increased dramatically after the Federal Interstate Highway Act passed in 1956, promising 41,000 miles of interstate highways that would link suburbs to cities. As a result, the number of new homeowners in the 1950s increased by an unprecedented 9 million people.

Americans' new materialism resulted from their eagerness to forget the hardships of the economic Depression of the 1930s and the war that dominated the 1940s. Now the focus was on obtaining a good white-collar job, marrying, and raising a family in a suburban home with a lawn and a backyard barbecue. As the workweek decreased to 40 hours, Americans enjoyed more leisure time for personal comfort and entertainment.

Attitudes toward class distinctions also changed during the 1950s. Many Americans echoed Ernest Hemingway's assertion that the only characteristic that set the rich apart from the rest of the classes was that they had more money. As more members of the middle class acquired the goods that had previously been reserved for the wealthy—the large shiny cars, the backyard swimming pools, the memberships to golf clubs—some class lines began to blur. Having (and spending) money lost the stigma it had had in the previous two decades when the wealthy had been criticized for lavish lifestyles in the face of depression and war. With the economy booming, the rich spent as they had in the twenties, and their habits were emulated by the burgeoning middle class. The introduction of department store and restaurant charge cards also helped ordinary Americans spend much as the rich did.

The growth of the materialistic middle class and the blurring of class lines sheds light on "A & P"—in particular on the characterizations of Sammy and the girls who come into the store. Sammy's small town may be poised on the brink of extinction as the clamor for suburban housing developments and shopping malls grows louder. Queenie and her friends are obviously part of this more affluent culture, yet Sammy's actions suggest that he believes he can bridge the gap between the classes.

THE AGE OF ANXIETY

Beneath the prosperous surface of American suburbia, tensions boiled. Galbraith's *The Affluent Society* as well as two other important studies noted that the rapid changes Americans were experiencing often left them confused and anxious. The titles of these works—*The Affluent Society, The Lonely*

Crowd and *The Organization Man*—became aphorisms that accurately characterized the pressures of the age. David Riesman, a sociologist at the University of Chicago, and a colleague, Nathan Glazer, argued in *The Lonely Crowd* (1950) that Americans had become "other-directed"—coerced to conform to social dictates set by politicians, religious leaders, and the media—instead of "inner-directed"—resisting outside pressures and maintaining individual values and beliefs. In other words, Americans had become too eager to fit into the community. Although this urge often resulted in surface unity and serenity, it could also produce underlying feelings of alienation and frustration, thus creating the sense of being alone in a crowd.

In *The Organization Man* William Whyte extended the argument against conformity in the community to the workplace, where corporate ethics demanded a similar devotion to the good of the group. Independence and self-expression were suppressed; adaptation was encouraged and rewarded. "Company men" were not only expected to think alike, behave alike, and dress alike, but their conformity was also required outside of work, where they were pressured to entertain, play golf, drink, and acquire a supportive and cooperative family who would help to ensure the success of the head of the household.

This pressure to conform to traditional values and beliefs emerges in the characterization of Lengel in "A & P" and in his interaction with Sammy. Sammy's reluctance to conform and become a "company man" will lead him to his final action in the story, an action that will alienate him from his workplace and possibly from his community.

THE COLD WAR

Another impetus for conformity emerged during the Cold War. Soon after World War II, when Russian leader Joseph Stalin set up satellite Communist states in Eastern Europe and Asia, the Cold War began, ushering in a new age of warfare and fear triggered by several circumstances: the United States's and the USSR's emergence as superpowers; each country's ability to use the atomic bomb; and Communist expansion and American determination to check it. Each side amassed stockpiles of nuclear weapons that could not only annihilate each country, but the entire world. Each side declared the other the enemy and redoubled its commitment to fight for its own ideology and political and economic dominance.

As China fell to the Communists in 1949, Russia crushed the Hungarian revolution in 1956, and the United States adopted the role of world policeman, the Cold War accelerated. In 1950, the United States resolved to help South Korea repel Communist forces in North Korea. By 1953, 33,629 American soldiers had been killed in the Korean War.

The Cold War induced anxiety among Americans, who feared both annihilation by Russians and the spread of Communism at home. Americans were encouraged to stereotype all Russians as barbarians and atheists who were plotting to overthrow the US government and brainwash its citizens. The fear that Communism would spread to the United States led to suspicion and paranoia, and many suspected Communists or Communist sympathizers saw their lives ruined. This "Red Scare" was heightened by the indictment of ex-government officials Alger Hiss in 1950 and Julius and Ethel Rosenberg in 1951 for passing defense secrets to the Russians. Soon, the country would be engaged in a determined and often hysterical witch hunt for Communists, led by Senator Joe McCarthy and the House of Representatives' Un-American Activities Committee (HUAC). By the time of McCarthy's death in 1957, almost six million Americans had been investigated by government agencies because of their suspected Communist sympathies, yet only a few had been indicted. (In 1954, McCarthy was censured by the Senate for his unethical behavior during the Committee sessions.)

This paranoid atmosphere provided Americans with another impetus for conformity. Many felt safety could be ensured only if they embraced the traditional values of church, home, and country. During this time, however, voices of protest began to emerge. Some Americans refused to succumb to the anti-Communist fervor and would not cooperate with the Senate hearings despite the threat of prison or exile from the United States. Others rebelled against a system that they thought encouraged discrimination and social and economic inequality.

THE CIVIL RIGHTS MOVEMENT

In the 1950s almost half of working white Americans enjoyed the comforts of middle class life, while the overwhelming majority of African-Americans struggled with the devastating realities of poverty. African-Americans wanted a good education and good jobs so they too could participate in the consumer society. America's official doctrine concerning civil rights was "separate but equal." Yet as long as blacks were denied the right to attend school, dine, travel, or work alongside whites, they had no chance of gaining any measure of equality. Most white Americans did not actively try to remedy this situation, but some began to protest racial segregation on the grounds that it could no longer be supported from a moral, religious, or legal standpoint.

During this decade, the stage would be set for the climactic civil rights achievements of the 1960s. In 1954 the Supreme Court ruling in Brown versus the Board of Education of Topeka, Kansas, outlawed "separate but equal" schools and made integration the law of the land. At the same time both blacks and whites worked to win racial tolerance and equal rights for blacks. Groups like the NAACP (National Association for the Advancement of Colored People) and the SCLC (Southern Christian Leadership Conference) encouraged nonviolent demonstrations against segregation. In 1955 Rosa Parks refused to give up her seat on a Montgomery, Alabama bus to a white passenger, triggering a year-long bus boycott by nearly 40,000 African-Americans that ended a year later when city officials finally accepted a court order to integrate transportation in the city. In 1960 four African-Americans, one of whom had been refused service there the day before, staged a sit-in at a Woolworth's lunch counter in Greensboro, North Carolina, an action that spurred similar sit-ins across the South. However, efforts to gain African-Americans their civil rights were often met with strong, even violent, resistance, and racial tensions escalated as white Americans tried to deny African-Americans the right for equality. In 1956 white students at the University of Alabama rioted against the court-ordered admission of the first African-American student; in 1957 President Eisenhower had to send federal troops to Little Rock, Arkansas, to ensure African-Americans' safety in white schools.

The undercurrent of rebellion that began to emerge in America during this period is reflected in the character of Sammy, who observes (and disapproves of) the constrained, conforming customers and workers at his supermarket. Through Sammy, Updike introduces a voice of dissent that refuses to compromise individual beliefs and values.

A Woman's Place

Women's roles in the 1950s changed more slowly than did those of racial minorities. During World War II, women were encouraged to enter the workplace where they enjoyed a measure of independence and responsibility. After the war, however, they were expected (and required) to give up their jobs to the returning male troops. Hundreds of thousands of women were laid off and expected to resume their roles in the home.

Training began at an early age to ensure that girls would conform to the feminine ideal and become the perfect wives and mothers. Women who tried to gain self-fulfillment through careers were criticized and deemed dangerous to the stability of the American family. They were pressed to find fulfillment exclusively through their support of a successful husband. Television shows (*Ozzie and Harriet, Father Knows Best*), popular magazines (*Good Housekeeping*), and advertisements all encouraged the image of woman-as-housewife throughout the '50s. The women who did work outside the home (by 1956, thirty-five percent of all American women) often suffered discrimination and exploitation as they were relegated to low-paying clerical, service, or assembly-line positions. Women would have to wait until the 1960s and '70s to gain meaningful social and economic advancement.

Sexuality

Traditional attitudes about sex began to change during this era. Dr. Alfred Kinsey's reports on the sexual behavior of men and women (1948, 1953) helped bring discussions of this subject out in the open. Although many Americans clung to puritanical ideas about sexuality, they could not suppress questions that began to be raised about what constituted normal or abnormal sexual behavior. The public was intrigued by movie stars like Marilyn Monroe and Brigitte Bardot, who openly flaunted their sexuality. *Playboy* magazine, launched in 1953, gained a wide audience. Hugh Hefner, publisher of the magazine, claimed that the magazine's pictures of naked women were symbols of "disobedience, a triumph of sexuality, an end of Puritanism." *Playboy* itself promoted a new attitude toward sexuality with its "playboy philosophy" articles and its centerfolds of naked "girls next door." In the 1960s, relaxed moral standards would result in an age of sexual freedom, but most Americans in the '50s retained conservative attitudes toward sexuality: they did not openly discuss sexual behavior, and promiscuity—especially for women—was not tolerated.

In "A & P" Sammy's attitudes toward women and sexuality reflect an ironic mixture of traditional and nontraditional views. Although Sammy becomes a voice of rebellion in "A & P," he also reveals his traditional attitude toward women. Queenie and her friends are objects to Sammy—objects to be admired for their sexuality and to be protected from harm. His frank description of his sexual attraction to Queenie in the repressed climate of the times, however, suggests his break with the status quo.

THE INFLUENCE OF THE YOUNG

By 1958 one-third of the US population was younger than fifteen. As a result, American politicians, manufacturers, and advertisers began to pay attention to teenagers' problems and interests. For most of the decade, young Americans followed in the path of their parents, sharing their ambitions to rise to (or stay firmly entrenched in) the middle class and succumbing to the pressure to conform in order to achieve that goal. Their political and social apathy prompted contemporaries to label them the "silent generation." However, tensions beneath the surface eventually left the young feeling disillusioned and confused and prompted a loss of faith in social and political institutions. In the next decade, the rebellion would become political, as college students began protesting the mistreatment of blacks, nuclear proliferation, and US involvement in the Vietnam War. Teenagers in the '50s focused on more personal issues as they struggled against conformity and strove to express their individuality. Their rebellion sometimes took the form of juvenile delinquency, which became a serious problem as youth crime increased. A less harmful, though initially just as socially objectionable, outlet was discovered as a new form of music—rock and roll—was born.

THE ROCK AND ROLL GENERATION

Young Americans embraced rock and roll music as an outlet for feelings of confusion and alienation and as an avenue for self-expression. Teens snapped up recordings by new black artists like Chuck Berry and Fats Domino, helping to propel these entertainers toward stardom. Parents resisted admitting into their suburban homes the voices of black singers (and white singers who sounded black), with their promotions of sexual experimentation and freedom from parental control. When these parents clashed with their rebellious children, a gap between the generations formed. Rock and roll stars, as well as the confused young rebels portrayed on the screen by actors like James Dean and Marlon Brando, usurped parental power and became the new role models for the younger generation.

Role models were also provided by the "Beats," a label that linked a group of avant-garde American writers who shared a disdain for traditional social values and political realities and promoted individuality, sexual freedom, and drug experimentation. Jack Kerouac's chronicle of the counterculture, *On the Road* (1957), and Allen Ginsberg's poem "Howl" (1956) became the defining works of the movement. Many young adults, especially those in college at the time, responded to Ginsberg's complaint that he "saw the best minds of his generation destroyed by madness" and imagined themselves "on the road" with Kerouac, rejecting the material comforts of suburbia in search of life's deeper meaning.

A New Decade

By the time Americans reached the 1960s, the foundation for change had been set. Traditional values and beliefs had been challenged and, to some degree, altered. When our new, vibrant young president encouraged us to "ask not what your country can do for you; ask what you can do for your country," many turned away from the materialism and apathy of the previous decade. When President Kennedy established the Peace Corps in 1961 so that young Americans could offer assistance and goodwill to struggling countries, 13,000 applications were received in the first year.

Yet, as Kennedy had noted in his acceptance speech after his election, "perils" and "threats" remained. In his inaugural address he pledged that the United States would "pay any price, bear any burden" to defend the free world, a promise that would be fulfilled in the devastation of the Vietnam War. Also, while some battles for equality had been won, racial tensions had not dissipated, as evidenced when riots broke out in 1960 in New Orleans as schools there tried to desegregate.

"A & P" does not deal explicitly with many of the issues that defined the 1950s and early 1960s. Still, in the story Updike plays out the conflict that arose in America at this time between those who called for conformity to traditional values and beliefs and those who inspired rebellions against them. Sammy confronts the conflicting urges of conformity and rebellion in himself and then faces the consequences of his choice, as did many Americans during this chaotic but exciting age.

WORKS CONSULTED

Barone, Michael. *Our Country: The Shaping of America from Roosevelt to Reagan.* New York: Free Press, 1990.

Brooks, John. *The Great Leap: The Past Twenty-Five Years in America.* New York: Harper, 1966.

Diggins, John Patrick. *The Proud Decades.* New York: Norton, 1988.

Duden, Jane. *1950s.* New York: Villard, 1993.

Galbraith, John K. *The Affluent Society.* Boston: Houghton Mifflin, 1958.

Halberstam, David, *The Fifties.* New York: Villard, 1993.

Jackson, Kenneth T. *Crabgrass Frontier: The Suburbanization of America.* New York: Oxford UP, 1985.

Johnson, Paul. *Modern Times: From the Twenties to the Nineties.* Rev. ed. New York: HarperCollins, 1991.

Kaufmann, Carl. *Man Incorporate: The Individual and His Work in an Organized Society.* Garden City, NY: Doubleday, 1967.

Kirk, Russell. *The Conservative Mind.* Chicago: Regnery, 1953.

Kowinski, William. *The Malling of America: An Inside Look at the Great Consumer Paradise.* New York: Morrow, 1985.

Layman, Richard, ed. *American Decades: 1950–1959.* Detroit: Gale, 1994.

Lewis, Peter. *The Fifties.* New York: Lippincott, 1978.

Low, David. *The Fearful Fifties: A History of the Decade.* New York: Simon & Schuster, 1960.

Lubell, Samuel. *Revolt of the Moderates.* New York: Harper, 1956.

Lukacs, John. *Outgrowing Democracy: A History of the United States in the Twentieth Century.* Garden City, NY: Doubleday, 1984.

———. *Passing of the Modern Age.* New York: Harper, 1970.

McCaffery, John K. M. ed., *The American Dream: A Half-Century View from "American Magazine."* Garden City, NY: Doubleday, 1964.

Miller, Douglas T. and Marion Nowak. *The Fifties: The Way We Really Were.* Garden City, NY: Doubleday, 1977.

Montgomery, John. *The Fifties.* London: Allen, 1966.

Whyte, William F. *The Organization Man.* New York: Simon & Schuster, 1956.

Zinn, Howard. *A People's History of the United States.* New York: Harper, 1990.

———. *Postwar America: 1945–1991.* Indianapolis: Bobbs-Merrill, 1973.

Literature

About the Author

JOHN UPDIKE (1932–), considered to be one of the most talented and prolific writers of his generation, has gained recognition for his work in four genres: the short story, the novel, poetry, and the essay. In his essays, Updike explores a wide range of subjects, ranging from a piece on Ted Williams's last baseball game for the Boston Red Sox to a critical examination of Hawthorne's works. Yet much of his fiction and poetry centers on the theme of loss—the loss of innocence, of love, of family, of religious faith, and in his more recent works, the inevitable loss of life. In his investigation of the detailed daily routines of middle-class Americans in small towns and suburbs, Updike illuminates the drama that can emerge from seemingly inconsequential moments.

Updike's settings are drawn from his own experiences with small-town life. He was born in Shillington, Pennsylvania and lived there until he was thirteen, when he moved with his family to a farm on the outskirts of that town. The loneliness he experienced on the farm often stimulated his imagination, as he has claimed, to dreams of "how to get out" of there. He left the farm when he won a scholarship to Harvard, where he worked as a writer and editor for *The Harvard Lampoon*. In 1954 he graduated summa cum laude with a degree in English, married, and moved to Oxford, England, where he studied at the Ruskin School of Drawing and Fine Arts on a Knox Fellowship.

His ambition during his school years was to be a cartoonist, but his first publication—a short story in *The New Yorker* titled "Friends from Philadelphia" in 1954—sidetracked those plans. When he returned from

Oxford, he began working at the magazine, often writing "Talk of the Town" columns. *The New Yorker* has been publishing his poems, stories, essays, and reviews regularly ever since. Updike quickly gained recognition after the publication of his first three books: a volume of poetry titled *The Carpentered Hen and Other Tame Creatures* (1958); the novel *The Poorhouse Fair* (1959); and *The Same Door* (1959), a collection of short stories.

His most critically acclaimed and most popular novels are the "Rabbit" quartet: *Rabbit, Run* (1960), *Rabbit Redux* (1971), *Rabbit Is Rich* (1981), and *Rabbit at Rest* (1990). These four novels chronicle Harry (Rabbit) Angstrom's middle-class suburban life from the somnolent '50s through the chaotic '60s and '70s to the egocentric '80s. Updike received the first of several awards for his work in 1959, when he won a Guggenheim Fellowship. Later he was awarded the Rosenthal Foundation Award of the National Institute of Arts and Letters for *The Poorhouse Fair;* the National Book Award in Fiction for his novel *The Centaur* (1963); O. Henry Awards for his short stories; the Pulitzer Prize, the National Book Critics Circle Award, and the American Book Award for *Rabbit Is Rich* (1981); the National Book Critics Circle Award for a collection of essays, *Hugging the Shore* (1983); and the Pulitzer Prize and the National Book Critics Circle Award for *Rabbit at Rest* (1990). He also was elected to the National Institute of Arts and Letters in 1964 and the American Academy of Arts and Letters in 1977.

"A & P" is Updike's best-known story and the one most often anthologized. It was first published in *The New Yorker* on July 22, 1961, and later in his short story collection *Pigeon Feathers* in 1962. The story, set in mid-century middle America, focuses on an incident in the life of Sammy, a nineteen-year-old checkout boy at the local supermarket. In his realistic depiction of a significant moment in this young man's life, Updike explores the tensions between the desire for freedom and the devotion to responsibility and the far-reaching consequences of acting on these urges.

A & P
(1961)

In walks these three girls in nothing but bathing suits. I'm in the third check-out slot, with my back to the door, so I don't see them until they're over by the bread. The one that caught my eye first was the one in the plaid green two-piece. She was a chunky kid, with a good tan and a sweet broad soft-looking can with those two crescents of white just under it, where the sun never seems to hit, at the top of the backs of her legs. I stood there with my hand on a box of HiHo crackers trying to remember if I rang it up or not. I ring it up again and the customer starts giving me hell. She's one of these cash-register-watchers, a witch about fifty with rouge on her cheekbones and no eyebrows, and I know it made her day to trip me up. She'd been watching cash registers for fifty years and probably never seen a mistake before.

By the time I got her feathers smoothed and her goodies into a bag — she gives me a little snort in passing, if she'd been born at the right time they would have burned her over in Salem — by the time I get her on her way the girls had circled around the bread and were coming back, without a pushcart, back my way along the counters, in the aisle between the check-outs and the Special bins. They didn't even have shoes on. There was this chunky one, with the two-piece — it was bright green and the seams on the bra were still sharp and her belly was still pretty pale so I guessed she just got it (the suit) — there was this one, with one of those chubby berry-faces, the lips all bunched together under her nose, this one, and a tall one, with black hair that hadn't quite frizzed right, and one of these sunburns right across under the eyes, and a chin that was too long — you know, the kind of girl other girls think is very "striking" and "attractive" but never quite makes it, as they very well know, which is why they like her so much — and then the third one, that wasn't quite so tall. She was the queen. She kind of led them, the other two peeking around and making their shoulders round. She didn't look around, not this queen, she just walked straight on slowly, on these long white prima-donna legs. She came down a little hard on her heels, as if she didn't walk in her bare feet that much, putting down her heels and then letting the weight move along to her toes as if she was testing the floor with every step, putting a little deliberate extra action into it. You never know for sure how girls' minds work (do you really think it's a mind in there or just a little buzz like a bee in a glass jar?) but you got the idea she had talked the other two into coming in here with her, and now she was showing them how to do it, walk slow and hold yourself straight.

She had on a kind of dirty-pink—beige maybe, I don't know—bathing suit with a little nubble all over it and, what got me, the straps were down. They were off her shoulders looped loose around the cool tops of her arms, and I guess as a result the suit had slipped a little on her, so all around the top of the cloth there was this shining rim. If it hadn't been there you wouldn't have known there could have been anything whiter than those shoulders. With the straps pushed off, there was nothing between the top of the suit and the top of her head except just *her,* this clean bare plane of the top of her chest down from the shoulder bones like a dented sheet of metal tilted in the light. I mean, it was more than pretty.

She had sort of oaky hair that the sun and salt had bleached, done up in a bun that was unravelling, and a kind of prim face. Walking into the A&P with your straps down, I suppose it's the only kind of face you *can* have. She held her head so high her neck, coming up out of those white shoulders, looked kind of stretched, but I didn't mind. The longer her neck was, the more of her there was.

She must have felt in the corner of her eye me and over my shoulder Stokesie in the second slot watching, but she didn't tip. Not this queen. She kept her eyes moving across the racks, and stopped, and turned so slow it made my stomach rub the inside of my apron, and buzzed to the other two, who kind of huddled against her for relief, and they all three of them went up the cat-and-dog-food-breakfast-cereal-macaroni-rice-raisins-seasonings-spreads-spaghetti-soft-drinks-crackers-and-cookies aisle. From the third slot I look straight up this aisle to the meat counter, and I watched them all the way. The fat one with the tan sort of fumbled with the cookies, but on second thought she put the packages back. The sheep pushing their carts down the aisle—the girls were walking against the usual traffic (not that we have one-way signs or anything)—were pretty hilarious. You could see them, when Queenie's white shoulders dawned on them, kind of jerk, or hop, or hiccup, but their eyes snapped back to their own baskets and on they pushed. I bet you could set off dynamite in an A&P and the people would by and large keep reaching and checking oatmeal off their lists and muttering "Let me see, there was a third thing, began with A, asparagus, no, ah, yes, applesauce!" or whatever it is they do mutter. But there was no doubt, this jiggled them. A few houseslaves in pin curlers even looked around after pushing their carts past to make sure what they had seen was correct.

You know, it's one thing to have a girl in a bathing suit down on the beach, where what with the glare nobody can look at each other much anyway, and another thing in the cool of the A&P, under the fluorescent lights, against all those stacked packages, with her feet paddling along naked over our checkerboard green-and-cream rubber-tile floor.

"Oh Daddy," Stokesie said beside me. "I feel so faint."

"Darling," I said. "Hold me tight." Stokesie's married, with two babies chalked up on his fuselage already, but as far as I can tell that's the only difference. He's twenty-two, and I was nineteen this April.

"Is it done?" he asks, the responsible married man finding his voice. I forgot to say he thinks he's going to be manager some sunny day, maybe in 1990 when it's called the Great Alexandrov and Petrooshki Tea Company or something.

What he meant was, our town is five miles from a beach, with a big summer colony out on the Point, but we're right in the middle of town, and the women generally put on a shirt or shorts or something before they get out of the car into the street. And anyway these are usually women with six children and varicose veins mapping their legs and nobody, including them, could care less. As I say, we're right in the middle of town, and if you stand at our front doors you can see two banks and the Congregational church and the newspaper store and three real-estate offices and about twenty-seven old freeloaders tearing up Central Street because the sewer broke again. It's not as if we're on the Cape; we're north of Boston and there's people in this town haven't seen the ocean for twenty years.

The girls had reached the meat counter and were asking McMahon something. He pointed, they pointed, and they shuffled out of sight behind a pyramid of Diet Delight peaches. All that was left for us to see was old McMahon patting his mouth and looking after them sizing up their joints. Poor kids, I began to feel sorry for them, they couldn't help it.

Now here comes the sad part of the story, at least my family says it's sad but I don't think it's sad myself. The store's pretty empty, it being Thursday afternoon, so there was nothing much to do except lean on the register and wait for the girls to show up again. The whole store was like a pinball machine and I didn't know which tunnel they'd come out of. After a while they come around out of the far aisle, around the light bulbs, records at discount of the Caribbean Six or Tony Martin Sings or some such gunk you wonder they waste the wax on, sixpacks of candy bars, and plastic toys done up in cellophane that fall apart when a kid looks at them anyway. Around they come, Queenie still leading the way, and holding a little gray jar in her hand. Slots Three through Seven are unmanned and I could see her wondering between Stokes and me, but Stokesie with his usual luck draws an old party in baggy gray pants who stumbles up with four giant cans of pineapple juice (what do these bums *do* with all that pineapple juice? I've often asked myself) so the girls come to me. Queenie puts down the jar and I take it into my fingers icy cold. Kingfish Fancy Herring Snacks in Pure Sour Cream: 49. Now her hands are empty, not a ring or a bracelet, bare as God made them, and I wonder where the money's coming from. Still with that prim look she lifts a folded dollar bill out of the hollow at the center of her nubbled pink top. The jar went heavy in my hand. Really, I thought that was so cute.

Then everybody's luck begins to run out. Lengel comes in from haggling with a truck full of cabbages on the lot and is about to scuttle into that door marked MANAGER behind which he hides all day when the girls touch his eye. Lengel's pretty dreary, teaches Sunday school and the rest, but he doesn't miss that much. He comes over and says, "Girls, this isn't the beach."

Queenie blushes, though maybe it's just a brush of sunburn I was noticing for the first time, now that she was so close. "My mother asked me to pick up a jar of herring snacks." Her voice kind of startled me, the way voices do when you see the people first, coming out so flat and dumb yet kind of tony, too, the way it ticked over "pick up" and "snacks." All of a sudden I slid right down her voice into her living room. Her father and the other men were standing around in ice-cream coats and bow ties and the women were in sandals picking up herring snacks on toothpicks off a big plate and they were all holding drinks the color of water with olives and sprigs of mint in them. When my parents have somebody over they get lemonade and if it's a real racy affair Schlitz in tall glasses with "They'll Do It Every Time" cartoons stencilled on.

"That's all right," Lengel said. "But this isn't the beach." His repeating this struck me as funny, as if it had just occurred to him, and he had been thinking all these years the A&P was a great big dune and he was the head lifeguard. He didn't like my smiling—as I say he doesn't miss much—but he concentrates on giving the girls that sad Sunday-school-superintendent stare.

Queenie's blush is no sunburn now, and the plump one in plaid, that I liked better from the back—a really sweet can—pipes up, "We weren't doing any shopping. We just came in for the one thing."

"That makes no difference," Lengel tells her, and I could see from the way his eyes went that he hadn't noticed she was wearing a two-piece before. "We want you decently dressed when you come in here."

"We *are* decent," Queenie says suddenly, her lower lip pushing, getting sore now that she remembers her place, a place from which the crowd that runs the A&P must look pretty crummy. Fancy Herring Snacks flashed in her very blue eyes.

"Girls, I don't want to argue with you. After this come in here with your shoulders covered. It's our policy." He turns his back. That's policy for you. Policy is what the kingpins want. What the others want is juvenile delinquency.

All this while, the customers had been showing up with their carts but, you know, sheep, seeing a scene, they had all bunched up on Stokesie, who shook open a paper bag as gently as peeling a peach, not wanting to miss a word. I could feel in the silence everybody getting nervous, most of all Lengel, who asks me, "Sammy, have you rung up this purchase?"

I thought and said "No" but it wasn't about that I was thinking. I go through the punches, 4, 9, GROC, TOT—it's more complicated than you think, and after you do it often enough, it begins to make a little song, that you hear words to, in my case "Hello (*bing*) there, you (*gung*) hap-py *pee*-pul (*splat*)!"—the *splat* being the drawer flying out. I uncrease the bill, tenderly as you may imagine, it just having come from between the two smoothest scoops of vanilla I had ever known were there, and pass a half and a penny into her narrow pink palm, and nestle the herrings in a bag and twist its neck and hand it over, all the time thinking.

The girls, and who'd blame them, are in a hurry to get out, so I say "I quit" to Lengel quick enough for them to hear, hoping they'll stop and watch me, their unsuspected hero. They keep right on going, into the electric eye; the door flies open and they flicker across the lot to their car, Queenie and Plaid and Big Tall Goony-Goony (not that as raw material she was so bad), leaving me with Lengel and a kink in his eyebrow.

"Did you say something, Sammy?"

"I said I quit."

"I thought you did."

"You didn't have to embarrass them."

"It was they who were embarrassing us."

I started to say something that came out "Fiddle-de-doo." It's a saying of my grandmother's, and I know she would have been pleased.

"I don't think you know what you're saying," Lengel said.

"I know you don't," I said. "But I do." I pull the bow at the back of my apron and start shrugging it off my shoulders. A couple customers that had been heading for my slot begin to knock against each other, like scared pigs in a chute.

Lengel sighs and begins to look very patient and old and gray. He's been a friend of my parents for years. "Sammy, you don't want to do this to your Mom and Dad," he tells me. It's true, I don't. But it seems to me that once you begin a gesture it's fatal not to go through with it. I fold the apron, "Sammy" stitched in red on the pocket, and put it on the counter, and drop the bow tie on top of it. The bow tie is theirs, if you've ever wondered. "You'll feel this for the rest of your life," Lengel says, and I know that's true, too, but remembering how he made that pretty girl blush makes me so scrunchy inside I punch the No Sale tab and the machine whirs "pee-pul" and the drawer splats out. One advantage to this scene taking place in summer, I can follow this up with a clean exit, there's no fumbling around getting your coat and galoshes, I just saunter into the electric eye in my white shirt that my mother ironed the night before, and the door heaves itself open, and outside the sunshine is skating around the asphalt.

I look around for my girls, but they're gone, of course. There wasn't anybody but some young married screaming with her children about some candy they didn't get by the door of a powder-blue Falcon station wagon. Looking back in the big windows, over the bags of peat moss and aluminum lawn furniture stacked on the pavement, I could see Lengel in my place in the slot, checking the sheep through. His face was dark gray and his back stiff, as if he'd just had an injection of iron, and my stomach kind of fell as I felt how hard the world was going to be to me hereafter.

Discussion Questions

1. Characterize Sammy using the background details he gives us about himself at the beginning of the story. How do these details help explain his actions?

2. What details does Sammy focus on that reveal his attitude toward his customers? Toward the girls? How do his attitudes toward them differ? Why?

3. Compare and contrast Sammy's and Stokesie's behavior. What social influences could explain the similarities and differences?

4. What kind of a person is Lengel? What motivates his actions? In what sense could he be seen as a foil for Sammy?

5. Are the girls responsible for what happens? Do you think they knew what problems might arise if they went into the store wearing bathing suits?

6. Why do you think Updike chose to set the story in a supermarket? Can you imagine other settings in which the story could take place?

7. Why does Sammy quit his job? Were any other options available to him?

8. Many critics regard the ending as ambiguous. Do you share Sammy's pessimism about his future, or are you more optimistic? Do you think quitting his job was a pointless gesture or a noble action?

9. What realities about his world does Sammy discover?

10. How might the story be different if it were told from Stokesie's point of view? From Lengel's? From Queenie's?

11. Watch the videotape of "A & P." Do the filmmakers present the setting and characters as you would have? Explain.

Research Questions

1. What do Sammy's actions reveal about his attitude toward women? Use the sources listed in the bibliography to discover in what respects his attitude was typical of the time period in which the story is set.

2. Critics have noted that Updike's work often includes a critique of American middle-class values. Do you think this statement is true of "A & P"? What particular values of the late 1950s and early 1960s seem to be embraced—and challenged—in the story?

3. This story can be regarded as a coming-of-age tale in that Sammy learns a good deal about himself and about what it means to be an adult. Use the sources collected in this Casebook to discover what others have said about this theme. Then, read a work of fiction by another author that focuses on a young adult learning about the responsibilities of life, and compare the themes in the two works. Are there significant similarities in what the two characters learn and how they learn it? In what ways are their situations and responses different?

4. Examine "A & P" alongside one or two other works by Updike. Use secondary sources to determine how much Updike's life and attitudes have influenced his themes, settings, and characterizations.

5. "A & P" is Updike's most frequently anthologized story. In an attempt to account for its continued popularity, survey the critical response to the story that appeared when it was first published. Why do you think it is such a popular choice for literature classes?

6. In an early draft of "A & P," Updike included a description of Sammy's actions after he quit his job. He later deleted this ending and expanded it into a story titled "Lifeguard" included in this Casebook. Examine the main character, setting, style, and themes in each story. What similarities and differences do you find? Compare your response to those offered in the secondary sources, including the section on "Lifeguard" in Luscher's article.

7. How have critics interpreted the closing words of "A & P," when Sammy admits, "I felt how hard the world was going to be to me hereafter"? What do they think Sammy means by "hard"? Do they agree or disagree with Sammy's assessment of his future? How do your responses to these questions compare with what the critics have written?

Secondary Sources

The twelve sources in this section* provide a variety of responses to "A&P" that can help you understand and write about the story. These sources include commentary on themes, characterization, setting, and style in "A&P" in particular as well as Updike's work in general. You may use these sources to help you generate your own ideas that can be developed into a paper about the story; you can also use critics' opinions to back up your own. The bibliography at the back of this book can help you locate future resources pertaining to Updike's life and works as well as information about the United States in the 1950s and early 1960s. Remember to document any words or ideas that you borrow from these and any other sources (see Appendix).

JOHN UPDIKE

Still Afraid of Being Caught

In a sense, all of life—every action—is a transgression. A child's undulled sensitivity picks up the cosmic background of danger and guilt. A child is in constant danger of doing something wrong. I was most severely punished, as I fallibly recall it, for being late in getting back home. At least once and perhaps several times my mother, her face red with fury, pulled a switch from the stand of suckers at the base of the backyard pear tree and whipped me on the backs of the calves with it, when I had been, let's say, a half-hour late in returning from the playground or some friend's house a few blocks away. Fear for my safety was, I suppose now, behind this stinging discipline, but at the time it seemed mixed up with her fear that, by playing late with some other boy, I would be on the road to homosexuality. She didn't like to

---

* Note that the Wells, Dressner, McFarland, and Porter articles do not use the parenthetical documentation style recommended by the Modern Language Association and explained in the Appendix.

see me wrestling with other boys, even on our own property. No doubt she was right, taking 'homosexual' in its broadest meaning, about young male roughhousing, but to my prepubescent self her anxieties seemed exaggerated. She didn't like to see my father, a 6-foot-2 schoolteacher with, as far as I could see, normal tendencies, put his hand on his hip either. But whatever the psychological roots of her (as I saw it, with eyes full of tears) overreaction, it did its work on my superego: I have an unconquerable dread of being late for appointments or returning home later than promised, and what modest heterosexual adventures were mine in adulthood received the slight extra boost, from deep in my subconscious, of my mother's blessing. Better this than one more game of Parcheesi over at Freddy Schreuer's, as the clock ticked sinfully toward 5:30.

We were Lutherans, and, as American Protestant denominations go, Lutherans were rather soft on transgression. In Luther's combative, constipated sense of the human condition, there was not much for it but to pray for faith and have another beer. This side of the cosmic background and of my mother's sexual preferences, I didn't really think I could do much wrong. Normal childhood sadisms—bug torture, teasing, fishing—repelled me, and I was all too thoroughly inclined to believe the best of my cultural-political context, from President Roosevelt down.

A child's transgressions are often, I believe, simple misunderstandings of how the world is put together. Once, attending a movie with my parents, I took the chewing gum from my mouth and put it on the seat where my father, a second later, sat, ruining forever (my impression was) the trousers of his new suit. The sense of a grievous financial mishap, verging on ruin, permeated the days afterward, and I had no answer to the question, Why did I do it? The answer seemed to be that I had wanted to get the chewing gum out of my mouth and had no sense of the consequences of my placing it on the seat beside me. I certainly meant my father no harm; he was mildness itself toward me, and an awareness of his financial fragility dominated our threadbare household.

Yet the other transgression that comes to mind also threatened him, though remotely, it appears now. Shillington, Pa., was a small town, where everything impinged. My father was a schoolteacher, and his domain began just beyond our backyard, across an alley and a narrow cornfield. The school grounds included the yellow-brick high school, several accessory buildings, a football field encircled by a cinder track, a baseball diamond with grass and wire backstop and bleachers, and a softball field that was little more, off-season, than a flat piece of dirt with a scruffy grass outfield. Early one spring, exulting perhaps in my March birthday, I was riding my fat-tired Elgin bicycle in this familiar terrain, alone, and thought to pedal across the dirt infield. I was stupidly slow to realize that the thawing earth was mud and that I was sinking inches down with every turn of the wheel. Within some yards, I could pedal no farther, and dismounted and walked the bike back to firmer terra; only then did I see, with a dull thud of the stomach, that I had left a profound, insolently wandering gouge in the infield, from beyond third base to behind the pitcher's mound. It looked as if a malevolent giant had run his thumb through the clay. I sneaked home, scraped the dried crust from my tires and hoped it would all be as a dream. Instead, my father began to bring home from school news of this scandal, the vandalized softball field. The higher-ups were incensed and the search for the culprit was on. He would be fired, I reasoned, if the culprit were revealed as his son, and we would all go to the county poorhouse—which, conveniently, was situated only two blocks away.

I forget how it turned out—my best memory is that I never confessed, and that the atrocious scar remained on the softball field until the advent of summer. How old was I? Old enough to propel a bicycle with some force, and yet so young that I did not grasp the elemental fact of spring mud. How blind we are, as we awkwardly push outward into the world! Such a sense of transgression and fatal sin clings to this (in its way, innocent) incident that I set down my confession with trepidation, fearful that the Shillington authorities will at last catch up to me, though I live hundreds of miles away, my father has been dead for more than 20 years and the last time I looked at the softball field it was covered with Astroturf.

ARTHUR MIZENER

Behind the Dazzle Is a Knowing Eye
(1962)

John Updike is the most talented writer of his age in America (he is 30 today) and perhaps the most serious. His natural talent is so great that for some time it has been a positive handicap to him—in a small way by exposing him from an early age to a great deal of head-turning praise, in a large way by continually getting out of hand. He has already written five books— two novels ("The Poorhouse Fair" and "Rabbit, Run"), a volume of verse ("The Carpentered Men"), and two books of stories ("The Same Door" and this book). Read in chronological order they show clearly the battle that has gone on between his power to dazzle and his serious insight.

His love of words and ideas for their own sake is almost Joycean, and he has often imitated Joyce in the almost mechanical way of someone doing an exercise in a creative-writing class: how his virtuosity must have charmed his writing teachers! His evident school-brightness and the first-class education it brought him provided every opportunity for the overdevelopment of his onomastic tendencies. They are most obvious in his verse ("Conceptually a blob, / the knob / is a smallish object which, / hitched / to a larger, / acts as verger"), but they are present also in his fiction, a constant pleasure to anyone who enjoys watching an artist at work.

Verbal brilliance of this kind, however, can be a danger for a writer of fiction. The young man who, under various names, is the hero of the stories in "Pigeon Feathers" says of one of his unknown rivals, "he would wear eyebrow-style glasses, be a griper, have some not quite negotiable talent, like playing the clarinet or drawing political cartoons," thus nicely illustrating his author's highly negotiable talent for adorning his stories with a cosmatesque surface of very great and radically irrelevant decorative charm. This lovingly executed, verbally elegant surface makes people describe Mr. Updike as a "poetic" writer, as indeed he is in a book like "The Poorhouse Fair." But charming as the poetry of "The Poorhouse Fair" is, Mr. Updike's preoccupation with it made him lose track of something he started to express in the book—that is, his sense of life itself—that is far more important than elegance.

This conflict between wit and insight stands out strongly in his early work because his insight, though it will stand romantic irony, cannot survive merely intellectual wit. It requires sincerity, even earnestness. Mr. Updike is a romantic; for him the instinctive, unselfconscious sense of "what feels right" is the source of life and the means to salvation. Rabbit Angstrom, the hero of "Rabbit, Run," may often inadvertently do harm, cause pain; but he is never evil or dead. "I don't know," he says to Ruth. "I don't know any of these answers. All I know is what feels right. You feel right to me. Sometimes Janice [his wife] used to. Sometimes nothing does."

Rabbit is touchingly inexperienced and naïve, but he has, as an old lady tells him, "Life. It's a strange gift and I don't know how we're supposed to use it but I know it's the only gift we get and it's a good one." When Rabbit, at the end of the book, runs away for the second time, it is a desperate and perhaps a futile act, but it is at least a continuation of the fight for life. Rabbit, run, is the author's imperative cry from the heart.

Mr. Updike is a romantic in a second sense which goes far to explain what has always been a curious source of strength in his work, his inclination to write almost exclusively about the life of a young man from the small Pennsylvania town he usually calls Olinger that seems very like the Shillington, Pa., that John Updike remembers from his own boyhood. Like all American romantics, that is, he has an irresistible impulse to go in memory home again in order to find himself. The epigraphs of his first book, which is dedicated to his parents, have to do with the importance of memory to desire and of family love, "within the light of which / All else is seen." The precise recollection of his own family-love, parental and marital, is vital to him; it is the matter in which the saving truth is incarnate.

Thus, in "The Persistence of Desire," Clyde Behn goes home to see an eye doctor and entangles himself with his childhood sweetheart, though they are both now married, with the result that "the maples, macadam, shadows, houses, cement, were to his violated eyes as brilliant as a scene remembered; he became a child again in this town, where life was a distant adventure, a rumor, an always imminent joy." Thus Allen Down in "Flight," remembering what looks like this same girl and his mother's jealousy of her, reconstructs a glowing world of details about his grandfather and grandmother (who turns up in several other stories), of school and classmates, of dances and debates. It is a meticulous, loving and beautiful re-creation, and Mr. Updike's mind probes it with the delicacy of a surgeon, seeking what makes it in memory seem "an always imminent joy."

Even the knowledge that it was not the shelter from nothingness that it now seems comes to him as a memory of how he got up his nerve to tell Mary Landis, the most mature and mysterious of his classmates, that he loved her, only to discover that she was having a bitterly unhappy love affair with an older man. "You never loved anybody," she said. "You don't know what it is." It is true. Now, he can remember what he thought then with a schoolboy's uncertain insight—"after all, it was just a disposition of his heart, nothing permanent or expensive; perhaps it was just his mother's idea anyway"—as true in a way he had not then been able to imagine.

It always seems to Mr. Updike, as he says of his grandmother, "necessary and holy to tell how once there had been a woman who now was no more," to tell everything, "all set down with the bald simplicity of intrinsic blessing thousands upon thousands of pages; ecstatically uneventful; divinely and defiantly dull." This conviction of the "unceasing and effortless blessing" of life when it is rightly apprehended makes Mr. Updike the kind of religious writer that every serious romantic must be.

The intensity with which he perceives this intrinsic blessing of life, however, seems to him incommunicable. Writers, he believes, "walk through volumes of the unexpressed and like snails leave behind a faint thread excreted out of [themselves]." These observations all come from "The Blessed Man of Boston, My Grandmother's Thimble, and Fanning Island," one of two experimental stories at the end of "Pigeon Feathers," in which Mr. Updike puts together three wholly unrelated episodes that seem to him images of life blessed, images that would be, if he could wholly invoke them, full of joy, "just as a piece of turf torn from a meadow becomes a *gloria* when drawn by Durer." But he despairs of realizing life that fully. "As it is," he tells the reader, "you, like me, must take it on faith."

This is not, of course, faith in the conventional sense; one should not be misled by Mr. Updike's frequent references to clergymen and church services; these are the accidents of his subject-matter, of the Olinger that he remembers. But a religious sense of the sacredness of life itself, with its accompanying sense of the absolute horror of death, is at the very center of his perception.

As he says in the almost too brilliant story, "Lifeguard," "Young as I am, I can hear in myself the protein acids ticking; I wake at odd hours and in the shuddering darkness and silence feel my death rushing toward me like an express train." The lifeguard of this story is concerned with the life of the spirit, and what he knows is that "every seduction is a conversion." "Someday," he believes, "my alertness will bear fruit; from near the horizon there will arise, delicious translucent, like a green bell above the water, the call for help, the call, a call, it saddens me to confess, that I have yet to hear." To have that vocation is to be saved by saving, by experiencing a love that is intensely and specifically physical, because "our chivalric impulses go clanking in encumbering biological armor."

This is the special significance of the second large group of stories in "Pigeon Feathers," the recollection of married love. Like the episodes of married love in "Rabbit, Run," they are unqualifiedly candid because they are dealing with the supreme moment, the moment at which the blessedness of life realizes itself, in the vivifying context of family life, with the maximum intensity—or seems, in memory, to have done so.

"Pigeon Feathers" is not just a book of very brilliant short stories; it is a demonstration of how the most gifted writer of his generation is coming to maturity; it shows us that Mr. Updike's fine verbal talent is no longer pirouetting, however gracefully, out of a simple delight in motion, but is beginning to serve his deepest insight, that his "Love's Labor's Lost" and even his "Romeo and Juliet" (that is "Rabbit, Run") are now behind him.

ROBERT M. LUSCHER

John Updike:
A Study of the Short Fiction
(1993)

"A&P," Updike's most frequently anthologized piece, is, on the surface, un-
characteristic. Sammy, the brash teenaged narrator, fashions a seamless narrative and fast-moving plot that is structurally distinct from the lyrical mood
or the much looser construction generally evident in Updike's short fiction.
A closer inspection of "A&P," however, reveals similar thematic concerns
and narrative techniques. Ringing up HiHo crackers rather than reading
Virgil, Sammy stands apart from the sensitive young men Updike habitually
portrays in his Olinger stories; he is closer in spirit to Ace Anderson of Updike's early story "Ace in the Hole." Yet his impulsiveness ultimately gives
way to a nascent awareness of the compromises that may be entailed on the
other side of the A&P's automatic door once he crosses through for the last
time. While the story lacks the ache of nostalgia present in many of the collection's other pieces, Sammy's backward glance at the recent past seeks its
full implications. In retelling the story, he refines the experience into a form
that will live in his memory, significant in its continuing impact on his life.
Like Walter in the preceding story, Sammy must wait until the initial dis-
turbance passes before his creatively enriched memory of the incident becomes one of the first "pricked moments" in the darkening sky of maturity.
"A&P" finally turns out to be another story of a character caught in the
middle between romance and realism, and beginning to learn the lessons of
bittersweet triumph.

Sammy's narrative, one of the nine first-person experiments in the volume, displays a surprising elasticity of tone, from the ungrammatical open-
ing sentence to the adolescent comparison between Queenie's breasts and
scoops of vanilla ice cream to more exact and poetic similes that may reveal
an embryonic writer (e.g., "shoulder bones like a dented sheet of metal tilted
in the light"). Sammy's lively verbal performance seeks to engage our sympathy for his individualistic gesture in a world of sheep-like shoppers and
his manager Lengel's prudish conventionalism. Retelling his story, he casts
himself in the role of the "unsuspected hero" that he fails to become for
Queenie and her friends. Yet in some respects, his bravado reveals the distance he still must travel toward true maturity. Though only 19, Sammy
condescendingly refers to one of Queenie's friends as a "kid"; near the end

of the story, however, we learn that Sammy's mother still irons his shirts. Nonetheless, he attempts to associate himself in the reader's mind with Stoksie, who is married, independent, and three years his senior; the only difference between them, he asserts, is the two children Stoksie has "chalked up on his fuselage already"—a testimony to his masculinity in Sammy's wishful vision.

In quitting his job, Sammy initially seeks to impress the three girls with a gesture that will establish his heroism as a masculine protector. Yet his attitude toward women is callow and chauvinistic: he likens the female mind to a "little buzz like a bee in a glass jar" and admires Queenie more for her body and social status than for her retort to Lengel. Furthermore, his disproportionate admiration of Queenie's 49-cent jar of Fancy Herring Snacks exhibits a basic social insecurity; to Sammy, this food is an exotic delicacy emblematic of a lifestyle beyond the reach of his parents (whose "racy" parties feature lemonade and Schlitz beer in stenciled glasses)—a lifestyle on which the ordinariness of the A&P has no right impinging. When Queenie speaks, Sammy "slid right down her voice into her living room," but the scene he imagines is a naive projection of his concept of the good life rather than a moment of genuine insight.

Sammy's shortcomings, however, must be weighed against the strides he makes during and after the experience. He may cling to adolescent attitudes and be motivated by the wrong reasons, but losing his job has at least spurred him to reconsider his position. Initially, he joins Stoksie in leering at the trio of girls in bathing suits, but he experiences a turning point in his feelings when, from his slot at the end of the meat counter, he watches McMahon, the butcher "patting his mouth and looking after them sizing up their joints. Poor kids, I began to feel sorry for them, they couldn't help it." Seeing the butcher assessing the girls like so much meat, as he himself was, awakens Sammy's pity and stirs some guilt; he still calls them "kids," but with an incipient awareness of their victimization. Whatever his faults, Sammy has an active imagination, a growing facility with language, and a perceptive eye and ear. While his defense of the girls may be motivated by a combination of lust, admiration for Queenie's social status, and sentimental romanticism, his gesture is not without principle and quickly assumes more serious overtones. His uncharitable assessments of Lengel and the customers show his growing distance from the world of the A&P; quitting merely severs whatever connection remains.

Yet the tenuous link he felt with Queenie and her world vanishes when she crosses the electric eye and Sammy remains to follow through on his actions; though he follows her across the threshold, he ends up alone in the parking lot, suspended between two inaccessible worlds. Instead of his dream girl, he is met with a premonition of the realities of married life: a young mother yelling at her spoiled children. While saved from the "injection of iron" that has made Lengel inflexible, Sammy realizes the truth of his last words: "You'll feel this for the rest of your life." Indeed, Sammy's recounting of the story shows him determined to do so; he refuses to stoop to self-pity and see its denouement as "the sad part," preferring instead to savor the incident's harsh lesson of "how hard the world was going to be on me hereafter" and thus prepare himself for its unforseen repercussions.

Ralph's plunge into the waters of guilt is followed by the egotism of the shore-bound narrator of "Lifeguard," who begins his dramatic monologue by declaring his virtue: "Beyond doubt, I am a splendid fellow." Updike's calculated ambiguity, resulting from the omission of the article from the more idiomatic phrase "beyond a doubt," immediately raises a number of questions, including whether this divinity student who works in the summer as a lifeguard is indeed beyond doubt, whether such a condition of absolute faith is possible, and whether the lifeguard's image of himself as a splendid fellow is an inflated illusion. Describing himself in glowing terms that recall the gifts in "Archangel," the lifeguard would have us believe he is a gift from God; indeed, in his rhetoric he implicitly likens himself to Christ, incarnated as a savior mounted on the tower with the red cross. Yet he inhabits a world of abstraction and prefers to remain aloof from the surrounding world. In this erudite sermon which teaches more about him than about the mysteries of faith, he muses on the nature of his calling and the modern world's problems of faith, but waits in vain to be called by a congregation of indifferent sunworshippers.

After his memorable parable of swimming as a search for faith, however, the promising introduction to his sermon on the modern inability to confront immensity becomes a condescending and sophistic justification of his lust. In an ironic echo of Kierkegaard's ideas about the man above the crowd of untruth, the lifeguard sets himself above his flock, criticizing every age group except the nubile young girls whose bodies make them more eligible candidates for his personal attention. He is merely a novice theologian who intellectualizes his lust and cloaks seduction with the veil of conversion. Indeed, a sexual overture, not a cry from someone who needs help venturing out into the sea of faith, may be the call he waits for in vain. While offered as a consolation to the masses, his final injunction to enjoy "the single everpresent moment that we bring to our lips brimful" stands out amidst his incoherent and self-serving theology as the suggestion of the world's sacramental nature—a message that should perhaps not be dismissed because of the elitism and narcissism of the messenger.

DONALD M. MURRAY

An Interview with John Updike
October 29, 1995

DONALD M. MURRAY: John Updike, how did this story come to you?

JOHN UPDIKE: Well, it was at a time in my life when I wrote a lot of short stories. I was really in the business of looking for ideas and I lived in a small New England town with my family and in driving by the local A&P I said to myself or my wife, "Why don't you ever read a story set in an A&P" or some other, not necessarily A&P, but A&P was the going brand name at the time and the natural title, it was a good title which is always a nice way to begin a short story, and I had seen some time before a single girl I think in the aisles of a supermarket wearing only a bathing suit and it was sort of shocking. It was a stunning effect, even though on the beach she would not have been, you wouldn't have given her a second glance. So this notion of the kind of the public nakedness in this commercial setting was where I began this story. Of course, you couldn't get too far with just that vision. I had to have a pro-tagonist and Sammy was it. And the voice, his voice, his sort of slangy voice, in walks these three girls in nothing but bathing suits and so on. And all that followed from my middle-aged vision, or my young mar-ried vision. I transposed all of my lustful and quizzical feelings onto this adolescent boy.

DONALD M. MURRAY: In what ways, if any, do you identify with Sammy? Did you work at a supermarket? Does he remind you of yourself at your age?

JOHN UPDIKE: Well, yes, I was once young. And in fact when I wrote this story I wasn't terribly old. If it was written in '61 I would have been just 29, so I was a kid myself, really, and certainly could remember what it was like to be 18 or 19. I never worked in a supermarket, no. The notion that he would be struck by these three girls in bathing suits certainly, I think almost any normal, adolescent male would have been struck.

DONALD M. MURRAY: What about Queenie? Could you tell us a little more about her?

JOHN UPDIKE: Well Queenie is meant to be the beauty of the three and it's really she who strikes him, and it's really on her behalf that he does his noble, his rebelignation, his noble surrender of his position; there is also this to be said about Queenie, that she appears to be coming, from what she buys, she buys little herring snacks and she talks of her parents. She is of a higher social level than he, so in some sense this is a blue-collar kid longing for a white-collar girl. There is an element of social inequality here and I wonder to what extent his gesture of quitting, is in a way, has to do with the fact that she is rich and he is poor, as he sees it.

DONALD M. MURRAY: At what point did you know that he was going to respond and quit, and know his life is going to change?

JOHN UPDIKE: Well, he's quitting in a hot flash, as in a moment of manly decisiveness and the thought does hang over his shoulder that his parents will not be pleased, just like Mr. Langle, his boss, is not pleased. But, for the moment at least, he's reposing in the confidence that he's doing the right thing. He has seen a kind of a wrong done. These girls have been embarrassed about being, after all, themselves. So I don't think he's too worried about the future at the moment. Although the very last phrase of the story indicates that the world is going to be harder to him hereafter. He does note he's kind of crossed a Rubicon of a kind.

DONALD M. MURRAY: Which way do you think that it will be hard for him?

JOHN UPDIKE: Well, I think the fact that he, in this small town at least, it will be known that he quit this job at the A&P and that kind of thing does not set well in a small town. Everything is known really, information is passed on and he'll be known, perhaps, as a quitter.

DONALD M. MURRAY: So it's a choice that we all have to make, every generation that might be made in a different setting, but it's a crucial choice.

JOHN UPDIKE: The choice being between serving a master who seems suddenly cruel and unethical and yes, whether you want to go along. How far you should play the game as is defined by the power structure. Yeah, I suppose that does recur and probably not so very differently from generation to generation.

DONALD M. MURRAY: Is anything in the story intentionally symbolic? Langle's name, for example, implies the legal system, laws, regularities. Sammy's name is so open and friendly. Are you conscious of these things the teachers talk about?

JOHN UPDIKE: You certainly have to wait until the characters, as Faulkner somewhere said, name themselves. I think that in one of his novels the character has no name and Faulkner replied that the character had never named himself. So you do kind of wait. I'm not sure it's always a fully conscious decision that can be translated into what teachers say. But sometimes they're right. In the case of Langle, my mother's boss when she was a shop girl, not a shop girl, she was a saleswoman at a department store in a nearby city, and her boss was Mr. Langle. And I can remember her coming home and saying Langle did this and Langle said that and so the name in my mind had a sort of ominous authority to it. Sammy, I don't know, it is as you say a friendly kind of innocuous kid's name in a way. Stokes, I think that indicates that he was an older man. He was a married man who had acquired the dignity of his last name becoming his name.

DONALD M. MURRAY: Have you imagined Sammy's life after the story ended?

JOHN UPDIKE: You know the story went on in the original version. It didn't end where it does in the final and correct version. But I had written about three or four pages in which he goes down to the beach. Having quit his job he has no reason not to go to the beach and look for these girls whose hero he has after all been. He's given up his employment for the sake of these girls and he goes down there and can't find them, and that was the way my story ended. And the editor of *The New Yorker*, my editor of *The New Yorker*, Bill Maxwell, thought that the story ended where it did and although I've never been too crazy about editors having creative suggestions, in this case I thought it was a good one, that the story really ends with his decision to walk out. What I then had left over from "A&P" were these four pages of kind of girl watching at the beach which I turned into another story called "Lifeguard" and I kind of expanded on that. So nothing was wasted.

DONALD M. MURRAY: What do you feel about our society? Is it still as sheeplike as it seemed to be when you wrote the story?

JOHN UPDIKE: It was pretty much, however it is of today, it certainly was true of the time. This was the late Eisenhower, early Kennedy years in which people by and large conformed and were expected to conform. But there were a few voices of descent being raised, Croak and Ginsberg, and others, James Dean, I don't know if he was. But anyway, there was this undercurrent of rebellion. Elvis Presley, of course, was the great symbol of something else, of not being quite so constrained. And Sammy's observations of the sheeplike behavior perhaps prepares him to behave in an unsheeplike way when he quits. He's almost saying, "I'm not going to be one of you sheep. I'm going to do the right thing," and then take the consequences.

DONALD M. MURRAY: How would you like the reader to see the story?

JOHN UPDIKE: Well, of course, I don't want to read the story for any of my readers. The writer writes and the reader reads. And in a sense there is always some ambiguity or some room for various responses to a story. But I certainly see him as a typical, well intentioned, American male trying to find his way into society, and full of good impulses. I think that he quit his job on a good impulse really, a kind of feminist protest in a way is what he does here and who knows what his adult life will bring, but I think for the moment he's a boy who has tried to reach out of his immediate environment toward something bigger and better.

DONALD M. MURRAY: You're aware of the boy's thought when you're writing, you hear the story, do you?

JOHN UPDIKE: Yeah. You're certainly aware. In these years I think most of my stories were written in a third person. So for me to embark upon a first person story, I certainly knew what I was doing and knew that I had to keep doing it once I'd started to do it.

DONALD M. MURRAY: Would you mind reading some of the story for us so we could hear your voice and the voice of the story?

JOHN UPDIKE: "In walks these three girls in nothing but bathing suits. I'm in the third checkout slot with my back to the door, so I don't see them until they're over by the bread. I stood there with my hand on a box of HiHo crackers, trying to remember if I rang it up or not. I ring it up again and the customer starts giving me hell. She's one of these cash register watchers. A witch about fifty with rouge on her cheekbones and no eyebrows and I know it made her day to trip me up. The girls had reached the meat counter and were asking McMahon something. He pointed, they pointed and they shuffled out of sight behind the pyramid of Diet Delight Peaches. All that was left for us to see was old McMahon patting his mouth and looking after them sizing up their joints. Poor kids. Now here comes the sad part of the story, at least my family says it's sad. But I don't think it's so sad myself. The store is pretty empty it being Thursday afternoon, so there was nothing much to do except lean on the register and wait for the girls to show up again. The whole store was like a pinball machine and I didn't know which tunnel they had come out of. After a while, they come around out of the far aisle. Queenie's still leading the way and holding a little gray jar in her hand. And I could see her wondering between Stokes and me, but

Stokesie, with his usual luck draws an old party in baggy gray pants who stumbles up with four giant cans of pineapple juice. So the girls come to me." He becomes their champion in a sense; "I quit," even though they don't know it. And that the story would end right there was entirely clear to me, it was a little bit that it went on and he began to look for them and of course never could see them. He had given up his bow tie and his good name for girls who then vanished on him. Yeah, it was sort of the way I originally saw it ending.

DONALD M. MURRAY: Story of our lives.

JOHN UPDIKE: Yeah. Story of our lives. Right, any good story should be to some degree the story of all of our lives.

DONALD M. MURRAY: Thank you John Updike. We appreciate your spending the time with us. We know that anybody that writes three pages a day, year after year, provides us with such good reading, wants to get back to work. We appreciate the time that you gave us.

JOHN UPDIKE: It was a pleasure. Thank you.

DONALD MURRAY

E-Mail to Tim Westmoreland
April 2, 1996
Subject: A&P

Tim:

Even at 71 and an established member of the middle-class—I own my own single-family home—I read Updike's story autobiographically. I worked in Miller's market in North Quincy, Mass. as a teen-ager and was agonizingly aware of who lived—literally—across the railroad tracks and up on the hill. We like to think of the United States as without classes but we are a class society and when I read that story, I again live my teenager awareness of class.

Yes, the girls were slumming but I think his action in quitting had significant implications for his life where theirs did not. Maybe I'm wrong. Maybe it is an indication that will be imprisoned in their class where he may escape his. Or is that my autobiography again?

I'm afraid the concern with names came from the director's interest more than mine.

When a piece of writing is successful—and this story always works for me—it becomes my story as much as the author's. My momentary visit to

Updike's store triggers a thousand memories—I see, smell, taste, feel, hear again my afterschool and week-end hours at Miller's Market and feel, within me, the hunger to escape my family, my social and economic position. His story becomes mine and mine his in the blending of thought and feeling we call literature.

<hr>

DONALD M. MURRAY

Amid Onions and Oranges, a Boy Becomes a Man
April, 1996

Recently I reread John Updike's classic short story "A&P," in which a teenage clerk makes a decision that will change his life, and as I enter Updike's small grocery in the 1960s I am transported to Miller's Market in Wollaston, where I worked almost 60 years ago.

I am stunned by the immediacy of my crash-landing into the past. I am 14 and my hands are learning to take two tucks in the grocery apron and twice wrap the ties around my waist. I am skinny again.

I smell the earthy odor of root crops, the sawdust on the floor, the blood dripping from a fresh-cut chicken, the Pall Mall cigarette that hangs from my lip, the mark of my passage—I then think—from boy to man.

My hands can tip the boxes on the sidewalk just right to display the oranges, potatoes, carrots, onions, apples I stack in rising rows. I know how to take a cleaver and split a great green Hubbard squash so Mrs. Deming will have 7 pounds in one piece, no more.

My legs know how to bend to lug a 100-pound bag of potatoes in from the shed or get my shoulder under a side of beef from the truck so I can stagger-carry it into the refrigerator and hang it on a hook.

Updike's prose has taken me not into his life but into my own. I again know how to mix meat, filler, spices for Scottish beef sausages and the tricks of this trade as I grind the sausage and feed it into the natural intestine casing, twisting off each sausage at just the right length.

How many trades I learned in that crowded little store with Mr. Miller, a giant who always wore rubber boots and a straw hat; tiny, bustling Mrs. Miller, who bossed the boss and us all; Marshall, their son; Mike, the butcher, who got so drunk every Saturday I often had to hold him up but who never, ever nicked a finger as his cleaver crashed down or his trimming knife—more than razor sharp—zipped around a roast.

I could still prop the hearing unit of an old-fashioned tall telephone on my shoulder and write an order.

And Mr. Miller taught the retailer's trade. When Mrs. Temple asks about the cabbage, I'm to look at Mr. Miller, turn away and whisper, "Not today. Try the beets."

She'll always trust me, Mr. Miller, master of deception, assures me. And when Mrs. Wheeler comes in and asks about the beets, I look at Mr. Miller and whisper, "Not today. Try the cabbage."

In weeks I have housewives who will buy only from me. I am so honest, so innocent, so young, so very trustworthy.

I am even allowed, in an emergency, to drive the truck to Quincy Market in Boston or to make deliveries—two years before I have a license. My leg still stretches to reach the brake.

And I become a grown-up, not when I light up another Pall Mall, go over to the diner with Mike the butcher and drink a mug of coffee, or even when I drive the truck to market.

I come close to being a grown-up when I see the secret list of those who owe the store so much that they are not allowed to charge anything—not a bottle of milk, not a loaf of bread. Our name is high on the list.

I become a grown-up when I discover that my mother, despite the list, has talked Mr. Miller into allowing her to charge against my 50-cents-a-day pay before I earn it.

I tell Mr. Miller not to allow her to charge against my salary. It is a close neighborhood, and Mr. Miller must know that Father brings home more money than most. I have to explain that Mother spends it on gifts for her friends and does not pay our bills.

I feel again the hot flush of shame and then the necessary coldness that allowed me, even at 14, to distance myself from my family.

But not to escape. Past and present merge. I did graduate from Miller's Market, clambered firmly into the middle class, living in, even owning a single-family home, mortgage paid off.

Reliving that day in Miller's Market when I betrayed Mother, I feel the need to protect her and the contradictory need to protect myself.

I read about the boy in the A&P and the very different decision he makes, and through the skillful magic of Updike's prose, I read my own story.

And although I am no Updike, the magic continues. As you read my story, many of you heard your own.

DONALD MURRAY

Subject: More "A & P"
April 8, 1996

Tim:

A few more comments.

As I think about Updike's story, I re-experience my relationship with unavailable girls. I was Protestant in a largely Irish Catholic city. In fact, most girls were not available because of virtue, economic or social status.

I do feel those girls were slumming, flaunting themselves, knowing they could not really be approached. And Sammy's chivalrous gesture is, of course, hopeless.

And yet, I think, in doing what he did he saved his soul.

JOHN UPDIKE

Lifeguard
(1965)

Beyond doubt, I am a splendid fellow. In the autumn, winter, and spring, I execute the duties of a student of divinity; in the summer I disguise myself in my skin and become a lifeguard. My slightly narrow and gingerly hirsute but not necessarily unmanly chest becomes brown. My smooth back turns the colour of caramel, which, in conjunction with the whipped cream of my white pith helmet, gives me, some of my teenage satellites assure me, a delightfully edible appearance. My legs, which I myself can study, cocked as they are before me while I respose on my elevated wooden throne, are dyed a lustreless maple walnut that accentuates their articulate strength. Correspondingly, the hairs of my body are bleached blond, so that my legs have the pointed elegance of, within the flower, umber anthers dusted with pollen.

For nine months of the year, I pace my pale hands and burning eyes through immense pages of Biblical text barnacled with fudging commentary; through multi-volumed apologetics couched in a falsely friendly Victorian voice and bound in subtly abrasive boards of finely ridged, pre-faded red; through handbooks of liturgy and histories of dogma; through the bewildering duplicities of Tillich's divine politicking; through the suave table talk of Father D'Arcy, Étienne Gilson, Jacques Maritain, and other such moderns mistakenly put at their ease by the exquisite antique furniture and overstuffed larder of the hospitable St. Thomas; through the terrifying attempts of Kierkegaard, Berdyaev, and Barth to scourge God into being. I sway appalled on the ladder of minus signs by which theologians would surmount the void. I tiptoe like a burglar into the house of naturalism to steal the silver. An acrobat, I swing from wisp to wisp. Newman's iridescent cobwebs crush in my hands. Pascal's blackboard mathematics are erased by a passing shoulder. The cave drawings, astoundingly vital by candlelight, of those aboriginal magicians, Paul and Augustine, in daylight fade into mere anthropology. The diverting productions of literary flirts like Chesterton, Eliot, Auden, and Green—whether they regard Christianity as a pastel forest designed for a fairyland romp or a deliciously miasmic pit from which chiaroscuro can be mined with mechanical buckets—in the end all infallibly strike, despite the comic variety of gongs and mallets, the note of the rich young man who on the coast of Judaea refused in dismay to sell all that he had.

Then, for the remaining quarter of the solar revolution, I rest my eyes on a sheet of brilliant sand printed with the runes of naked human bodies. That there is no discrepancy between my studies, that the texts of the flesh complement those of the mind, is the easy burden of my sermon.

On the back rest of my lifeguard's chair is painted a cross—true, a red cross, signifying bandages, splints, spirits of ammonia, and sunburn unguents. Nevertheless, it comforts me. Each morning, as I mount into my chair, my athletic and youthfully fuzzy toes expertly gripping the slats that make a ladder, it is as if I am climbing into an immense, rigid, loosely fitting vestment.

Again, in each of my roles I sit attentively perched on the edge of an immensity. That the sea, with its multiform and mysterious hosts, its savage and senseless rages, no longer comfortably serves as a divine metaphor indicates how severely humanism has corrupted the apples of our creed. We seek God now in flowers and good deeds, and the immensities of blue that surround the little scabs of land upon which we draw our lives to their unsatisfactory conclusions are suffused by science with vacuous horror. I myself can hardly bear the thought of stars, or begin to count the mortalities of coral. But from my chair the sea, slightly distended by my higher perspective, seems a misty old gentleman stretched at his ease in an immense armchair which has for arms the arms of this bay and for an antimacassar the freshly laundered sky. Sailboats float on his surface like idle and unrelated but bene-volent thoughts. The soughing of the surf is the rhythmic lifting of his ripple-stitched vest as he breathes. Consider. We enter the sea with a shock; our skin and blood shout in protest. But, that instant, that leap, past, what do we find? Ecstasy and buoyance. Swimming offers a parable. We struggle and thrash, and drown; we succumb, even in despair, and float, and are saved.

With what timidity, with what a sense of trespass, do I set forward even this obliquely a thought so official! Forgive me. I am not yet ordained; I am too disordered to deal with the main text. My competence is marginal, and I will confine myself to the gloss of flesh with which this particular margin, this one beach, is annotated each day.

Here the cinema of life is run backwards. The old are the first to arrive. They are idle, and have lost the gift of sleep. Each of our bodies is a clock that loses time. Young as I am, I can hear in myself the protein acids tick-ing; I wake at odd hours and in the shuddering darkness and silence feel my death rushing towards me like an express train. The older we get, the fewer the mornings left to us, the more deeply dawn stabs us awake. The old ladies wear wide straw hats and, in their hats' shadows, smiles as wide, which they bestow upon each other, upon salty shells they discover in the morning-smooth sand, and even upon me, downy-eyed from my night of dissipation. The gentlemen are often incongruous; withered white legs support brazen barrel chests, absurdly potent, bustling with white froth. How these old roost-ers preen on their 'condition'! With what fatuous expertness they swim in the icy water—always, however, prudently parallel to the shore, at a depth no greater than their height.

Then come the middle-aged, burdened with children and aluminum chairs. The men are scarred with the marks of their vocation—the red fore-arms of the gasoline-station attendant, the pale X on the back of the overall-wearing mason or carpenter, the clammer's nicked ankles. The hair on their bodies has as many patterns as matted grass. The women are wrinkled but fertile, like the Iraqi rivers that cradled the seeds of our civilization. Their children are odious. From their gaunt faces leer all the vices, the greeds, the grating urgencies of the adult, unsoftened by maturity's reticence and fa-tigue. Except that here and there, a girl, the eldest daughter, wearing a knit suit striped horizontally with green, purple, and brown, walks slowly, care-fully, puzzled by the dawn enveloping her thick smooth body, her waist not yet nipped but her throat elongated.

Finally come the young. The young matrons bring fat and fussing in-fants who gobble the sand like sugar, who toddle blissfully into the surf and bring me bolt upright on my throne. My whistle tweets. The mothers rouse.

Many of these women are pregnant again, and sluggishly lie in their loose suits like cows tranced in a meadow. They gossip politics, and smoke incessantly, and lift their troubled eyes in wonder as a trio of flatstomached nymphs parades past. These maidens take all our eyes. The vivacious redhead, freckled and white-footed, pushing against her boy and begging to be ducked; the solemn brunette, transporting the vase of herself with held breath; the dimpled blonde in the bib and diapers of her Bikini, the lambent fuzz of her midriff shimmering like a cat's belly. Lust stuns me like the sun.

You are offended that a divinity student lusts? What prigs the unchurched are. Are not our assaults on the supernatural lascivious, a kind of indecency? If only you knew what de Sadian degradations, what frightful psychological spelunking, our gentle transcendentalist professors set us to, as preparation for our work, which is to shine in the darkness.

I feel that my lust makes me glow; I grow cold in my chair, like a torch of ice, as I study beauty. I have studied much of it, wearing all styles of bathing suit and facial expression, and have come to this conclusion: a woman's beauty lies, not in any exaggeration of the specialized zones, nor in any general harmony that could be worked out by means of the *sectio aurea* or a similar aesthetic superstition; but in the arabesque of the spine. The curve by which the back modulates into the buttocks. It is here that grace sits and rides a woman's body.

I watch from my white throne and pity women, deplore the demented judgement that drives them towards the braggart muscularity of the mesomorph and the prosperous complacence of the endomorph when it is we ectomorphs who pack in our scrawny sinews and exacerbated nerves the most intense gift, the most generous shelter, of love. To desire a woman is to desire to save her. Anyone who has endured intercourse that was neither predatory nor hurried knows how through it we descend, with a partner, into the grotesque and delicate shadows that until then have remained locked in the most guarded recess of our soul: into this harbour we bring her. A vague and twisted terrain becomes inhabited; each shadow, touched by the exploration, blooms into a flower of act. As if we are an island upon which a woman, tossed by her labouring vanity and blind self-seeking, is blown, and there finds security, until, an instant before the anticlimax, Nature with a smile thumps down her trump, and the island sinks beneath the sea.

There is great truth in those motion pictures which are slandered as true neither to the Bible nor to life. They are—written though they are by demons and drunks—true to both. We are all Solomons lusting for Sheba's salvation. The God-filled man is filled with a wilderness that cries to be populated. The stony chambers need jewels, furs, tints of cloth and flesh, even though, as in Samson's case, the temple comes tumbling. Women are an alien race of pagans set down among us. Every seduction is a conversion. Who has loved and not experienced that sense of rescue? It is not true that our biological impulses are tricked out with ribands of chivalry; rather, our chivalric impulses go clanking in encumbering biological armour. Eunuchs love. Children love. I would love.

My chief exercise, as I sit above the crowds, is to lift the whole mass into immortality. It is not a light task; the throng is so huge, and its members so individually unworthy. No *memento mori* is so clinching as a photograph of a vanished crowd. Cheering Roosevelt, celebrating the Armistice, there it is, wearing its ten thousand straw hats and stiff collars, a fearless and wooden-faced bustle of life: it is gone. A crowd dies in the street like a derelict; it leaves no heir, no trace, no name. My own persistence beyond the last rim of time is easy to imagine; indeed, the effort of imagination lies the other way—to conceive of my ceasing. But when I study the vast tangle of humanity that blackens the beach as far as the sand stretches, absurdities crowd in on me. Is it as maiden, matron, or crone that the females will be eternalized? What will they do without children to watch and gossip to exchange? What of the thousand deaths of memory and bodily change we endure—can each be redeemed at a final Adjustments Counter? The sheer numbers involved make the mind scream. The race is no longer a tiny clan of simian aristocrats lording it over an ocean of grass; mankind is a plague racing like fire across the exhausted continents. This immense clot gathered on the beach, a fraction of a fraction—can we not say that this breeding swarm is its own immortality and end the suspense? The beehive in a sense survives; and is each of us not proved to be a hive, a galaxy of cells each of whom is doubtless praying, from its pew in our thumbnail or oesophagus, for personal resurrection? Indeed, to the cells themselves cancer may seem a revival of faith. No, in relation to other people oblivion is sensible and sanitary.

This sea of others exasperates and fatigues me most on Sunday mornings. I don't know why people no longer go to church—whether they have lost the ability to sing or the willingness to listen. From eight thirty onwards they crowd in from the parking lot, ants each carrying its crumb of baggage, until by noon, when the remote churches are releasing their gallant and gaily dressed minority, the sea itself is jammed with hollow heads and thrashing arms like a great bobbing backwash of rubbish. A transistor radio somewhere in the sand releases in a thin, apologetic gust the closing peal of a transcribed service. And right here, here at the very height of torpor and confusion, I slump, my eyes slit, and the blurred forms of Protestantism's errant herd seem gathered by the water's edge in impassioned poses of devotion. I seem to be lying dreaming in the infinite rock of space before Creation, and the actual scene I see is a vision of impossibility: a Paradise. For had we existed before the gesture that split the firmament, could we have conceived of our most obvious possession, our most platitudinous blessing, the moment, the single ever-present moment that we perpetually bring to our lips brimful?

So: be joyful. Be Joyful is my commandment. It is the message I read in your jiggle. Stretch your skins like pegged hides curing in the miracle of the sun's moment. Exult in your legs' scissoring, your waist's swivel. Romp; eat the froth; be children. I am here above you; I have given my youth that you may do this. I wait. The tides of time have treacherous under-currents. You are borne continually towards the horizon. I have prepared myself; my muscles are instilled with everything that must be done. Someday my alertness will bear fruit; from near the horizon there will arise, delicious, translucent, like a green bell above the water, the call for help, the call, a call, it saddens me to confess, that I have yet to hear.

WALTER WELLS

John Updike's "A & P": A Return Visit to Araby
1993

John Updike's penchant for appropriating great works of literature and giving them contemporary restatement in his own fiction is abundantly documented—as is the fact that, among his favorite sources, James Joyce looms large.[1]

---

[1] Among the numerous critical acknowledgments of Updike's debt to Joyce's fiction, two of the most stimulating are by Mizener ("Behind the Dazzle is a Knowing Eye") and Joyce Carol Oates. Updike himself has examined Joyce's fictional aesthetic in his *New Yorker* article, "Questions Concerning Giacomo," a piece in which he suggests that nowhere are Joyce's characters better presented than in *Dubliners*. Among other writers in whose work Updike has found fertile source material for contemporary restatement, the most significant in recent years has been Nathaniel Hawthorne. Three of Updike's novels, *A Month of Sundays* (1975), *Roger's Version* (1986), and *S.* (1988) have been "retellings" of *The Scarlett Letter*, from the standpoints of Arthur Dimmesdale, Roger Chillingworth and Hester Prynne,

With special affinity for *Dubliners*, Updike has, by common acknowledgment, written at least one short story that strongly resembles the acclaimed "Araby," not only in plot and theme, but in incidental detail. That story, the 1960 "You'll Never Know, Dear, How Much I Love You"—like "Araby"—tells the tale of a poor, romantically infatuated young boy who, though obstructed by parental slowness, journeys with innocent urgency, coins in hand, to a seemingly magical carnival—only to find there, behind its facades, just a sleazy, money grasping, sexually tinged reality that frustrates and embitters him. Both stories draw on the Christian imagery of Bunyan's Vanity Fair episode to trace a modern boy's passage from innocence to experience, and to expose some of the pains and complexities of that passage. Notwithstanding "Araby"'s cachet as one of the great short stories in the English language, at least two critics have found "You'll Never Know, Dear" to be "a far more complex story."[2]

What remains unacknowledged, I think, is that shortly after writing "You'll Never Know, Dear," Updike made a second fictional excursion to Araby. This time he transformed Joyce's latter-day Vanity Fair, not into a cheaply exotic destination for a starry-eyed youngster, but into the richly resonant single setting for an older adolescent's sad tale: a tale of the modern supermarket. The resulting story, since its publication in 1962, has been Updike's most frequently anthologized: the popular "A&P." Updike even signals his intention for us at the outset, giving his story a title that metrically echoes Joyce's: Araby . . . A&P. (Grand Union or Safeway would not suffice.)

Like "Araby," "A&P" is told after the fact by a young man now much the wiser, presumably, for his frustrating infatuation with a beautiful but inaccessible girl whose allure excites him into confusing his sexual impulses for those of honor and chivalry. The self-delusion in both cases leads quickly to an emotional fall.

At 19, Updike's protagonist, Sammy, is a good bit older than Joyce's— at the opposite end of adolescence, it would seem. While in Joyce's boy we readily believe such confusion between the gallant and profane, I think we needn't assume that Sammy is likewise unable to distinguish between the two quite normal impulses. His attraction to the girl in the aisle is certainly far

---

respectively. An insightful discussion of these "Scarlet Letter" novels of Updike's is that by James A. Schiff.

[2] Hamilton 21–22. Another critic who perceptively explores the similarities between "You'll Never Know, Dear" and "Araby" is Robert Detweiler (8–9, 51–53).

more anatomically and less ambiguously expressed than that of Joyce's boy to Mangan's sister. But it is Beauty that confounds the issue. When human aesthetics come into play, when the object of a young man's carnal desire also gratifies him aesthetically, that is when the confusion arises. In Irish-Catholic Dublin of the 1890s,[3] such youthful beauty not surprisingly invokes analogies between Mangan's sister and the Queen of Heaven (though the swinging of her body and "the soft rope of her hair toss[ing] from side to side" [Joyce 30]), which captivate the boy, hint at something less spiritual than Madonna worship. And while beauty's benchmarks in Sammy's more secular mid-century America *are* more anatomical than spiritual, Updike does have Sammy call his young *femme fatal* "Queenie," and he does make her the center of a "trinity" of sorts, showing her two friends at one point "huddl[ing] against her for relief" ("A&P" 189).

Once smitten, both young protagonists become distracted, agitated, disoriented. Joyce's turns impatient "with the serious work of life" (Joyce 32). His teacher accuses him of idling. His heart leaps, his thoughts wander, his body responds "like a harp" to the words and gestures of Mangan's sister, which run "like fingers . . . upon the wires." (31) Similarly, Updike's young hero can't remember, from the moment he spots Queenie in the aisle, which items he has rung up on the cash register.

Even details in the two stories are similar, Updike clearly taking his cues from "Araby." Both boys are excited by specified *whiteness* about the girls—Joyce's boy by "the white curve of her neck" and "the white border of [her] petticoat" in the glow of Dublin lamplight (Joyce 32), Sammy by the "long white prima-donna legs" ("A&P" 188) and the white shoulders to which he refers repeatedly. "Could [there]," he wonders, "have been anything whiter than those shoulders[?]" (189). Joyce's boy also observes a nimbus surrounding Mangan's sister, "her figure defined by the light from the half-opened door" (30). True, Mangan's sister comports herself more humbly than her American counterpart. Queenie walks, heavy-heeled and head high, with the haughty pride of the affluent, secularized American upper middle class. But her enticing whiteness, in Updike's sly parody, is also given a luminous, halo-like quality: "around the top of the cloth," says Sammy of the bathing suit that "had slipped a little on her . . . there was this shining rim." (189)

---

[3] Though the story's events are not expressly dated in the narrative, the actual Araby bazaar—staged as a charity event to aid the Jervis Street Hospital in Dublin—fixes the story's climax at somewhere between 14 and 19 May 1894.

Both girls, remote as they are from their ardent admirers, also engage in some subtly seductive posturing. In the supermarket aisle, Queenie turns so slowly that Sammy's stomach is made to "rub the inside of [his] apron" (189). It's the same sensation, we suspect, that Joyce's protagonist feels when Mangan's sister "turn[s the] silver bracelet round and round her wrist" (Joyce 32) and bows her head toward him in the lamplight in front of her door. Queenie bows to no one, but the "clear bare plane of the top of her chest . . . [is] like a dented sheet of metal tilted in the light" ("A&P" 189). Her beauty, too, like that of Mangan's sister, is incandescent as it inclines toward her aspiring young knight.

Certainly one artistic motive for Updike's second reworking of "Araby" must be to contrast the spiritual value-systems and the adolescent sexual folkways of Joyce's Dublin with those of suburban New England in the Atomic Age. (The disillusionment of little Ben, who is only ten in "You'll Never Know, Dear," is clearly presexual.) "A&P" holds the secular materialism of Updike's own day up for comparison against the slowly imploding, English-dominated Irish Catholicism of the mid-1890s—and, behind it, the fervor of Protestant evangelism in Bunyan's seventeenth century. As critics have often noted, few non-Catholic writers in America make issues of religious faith and doubt as important in their fictions as does Updike.[4] In Victorian Dublin, redolent with the musty odor of incense, parochial schools, and the litter of dead priests, the Araby bazaar, a romanticized, pseudo-Oriental pavilion created by the fund raisers of the Jervis Street Hospital, stands incongruously pagan and temporary. It is there briefly, soon to be gone. Updike's supermarket, on the other hand, is permanently planted in the light of day near Boston, precisely where the church used to be: "right in the middle of town." "[From its] front doors," says Sammy, "you can see two banks and the Congregational church and the newspaper store and three real estate offices . . ." (191)—quite the satellites to material abundance they've become. The temple of modern consumerism has supplanted the house of worship at the heart of things. It is also an era in which Sammy (and hardly Sammy alone) takes for granted that the godless communists will take control sooner or later (as the British had long since assumed control in Joyce's Ireland). Sammy looks ahead quite assuredly to a time when the A&P (the Great Atlantic and Pacific Tea Co., that bedrock American

---

[4] For useful views of Updike's treatment of religious issues, see Yates 469–74 and Strandberg 157–75.

institution) will be "called the Great Alexandrov and Petrooshki Tea Company or something" (191).

Updike heightens the story's skepticism over the destiny of American Christianity by having his three girls stroll through the aisles of the A&P inappropriately clad, in reductive parody of Bunyan's pilgrims in Vanity Fair:

[E]ven as they entered into the fair, all the people in the fair were moved, and the town it self as it were in a Hubbub about them; and that for several reasons: For, First, the pilgrims were cloathed with such kind of Raiment as was diverse from the Raiment of any that Traded in that fair. The people therefore of the fair made a great gazing upon them. Some said they were fools, some they were Bedlams, and some they are Outlandish-men. (Bunyan 111)

The sheep pushing their carts down the aisle—the girls were walking against the usual traffic . . .—were pretty hilarious. You could see them, when Queenie's white shoulders dawned on them, kind of jerk, or hop, or hiccup, but their eyes snapped back to their own baskets and on they pushed. I bet you could set off dynamite in an A&P and the people would by and large keep reaching and checking oatmeal off their lists. . . . But there was no doubt this jiggled them. A few houseslaves in pin curlers even looked around after pushing their carts past to make sure what they had seen was correct. ("A&P" 190)

Contrast these two sets of "pilgrims" in the marketplace. Bunyan's proudly ignore exhortations that they partake of the bounty of the fair, insisting instead that the wares of the marketplace are nothing but stimuli to vanity. They will, they say, buy only the Truth. Queenie and her pals, on the other hand, do buy: one jar of Kingfish Fancy Herring Snacks in Pure Sour Cream.[5]

Queenie's approach to the checkout stand, Sammy warns us, begins "the sad part of the story" (192). Lengel, the store's manager, a self-appointed moral policeman who also teaches Sunday school, confronts the girls at the register—just as Bunyan's pilgrims are confronted by "the Great One of the fair" (i.e., Beelzebub; Bunyan 112). "Girls, this isn't the beach," Lengel tells

---

[5] The symbolism here is tantalizing. Is it Christ the king of fishermen we are meant to recall, reduced in this modern temple of consumerism to a tasty but soured snack that replaces the Truth alone that Bunyan's pilgrims will buy? Or should we infer an image of the legendary, impotent Fisher King of Arthurian legend, presiding over his wasteland?—so important symbolically to Eliot's great poem. Queenie's purchase seems to me the most symbolically provocative element in Updike's story.

them ("A&P" 193), echoing the Devil's demand in Vanity Fair that the pilgrims account for "what they did there in such an unusual Garb" (Bunyan 112). Queenie and her friends, like Bunyan's pilgrims, protest that they "weren't . . . shopping" ("A&P" 194), only buying the snacks that Queenie's mother asked them to get on their way home from the beach. Bunyan's pilgrims explain to *their* inquisitor that they are just passing through on their way to the Heavenly Jerusalem. Sammy imagines, in fact, that the girls *are* returning to their own latter-day heavenly city, the affluent beach set where folks eat "herring snacks on toothpicks off a big glass plate and . . . [hold] drinks the color of water with olives and sprigs of mint in them" (193)—this by comparison to the lemonade and Schlitz beer crowd, whence Sammy comes, where the suds are drunk from glasses with stenciled cartoons. In Bunyan's world, the choice was earthly vanity or heavenly salvation; in Updike's, it's just one level of class vanity or another.

To Queenie's protest, Lengel replies that it "makes no difference. . . . We want you decently dressed when you come in here." Queenie snaps back, insisting that she and her friends "*are* decent" (194). But they are nonetheless (after Lengel allows Sammy to ring up the herring snacks) quietly banished from the store. Bunyan's pilgrims, of course, are more harshly persecuted, thrown in a cage and forced to assert their dignity much more protractedly than Updike's girls. The difference, however, is only one of degree.

At the checkout stand, Sammy witnesses Queenie's mortification up close with profound, if complicated, sympathy. He tenderly unfolds the dollar bill she hands him ("it just having come," he says, "from between the two smoothest scoops of vanilla I had ever known" [193–94]), puts her change "into her narrow pink palm," hands her the jar of herring in a bag, then blurts out "I quit"—quickly enough, he hopes, for the girls to hear, so they will stop and acknowledge "their unsuspected hero" (194).

It's pure impetuousness on Sammy's part, a gallant gesture, a promise of sorts. Like Joyce's boy in Dublin, when face to face with the object of his adoration, not knowing what else to say or do, Sammy offers a gift. Where the Irish boy, in his comparatively poor working-class milieu, wants (perhaps needs) to offer something material to Mangan's sister to show his adoration, Sammy, who inhabits an affluent American world cut loose from the consolations of Christian faith, a world of largely material values, offers instead an assertion of principle as his gift. His Queenie has been wronged, and he will stand by her; in an age when the supermarket has replaced the church as the community's central institution, "principle" is the nearest equivalent one has to spiritual commitment. But before we anoint Sammy's act as one of pure principle, however imprudent, we should ask ourselves whether he would have done the same had one of the other girls—maybe Big Tall Goony-Goony—borne the brunt of the reprimand, with Queenie out of the picture. I doubt it.

The promises of both young men prove futile, of course. Joyce's boy gets to Araby too late, and recognizes in the flirtatious banter there between the salesgirl and her two English admirers, and in the two men counting money, something uncomfortably close to the nature of his own longing: his dream, he later sees, was actually sexual, and money would not buy it. In the A&P, Queenie and her friends disappear out the door. Sammy's promise is also in vain; but, like Joyce's young protagonist, he's stuck with it. "It seems to me," says Sammy, "that once you begin a gesture it's fatal not to go through with it" (196). He removes his apron and bow tie, and leaves the market. Once outside, he looks back woefully through the store windows and sees Lengel replacing him behind the cash register. Business goes on, and—as at Araby—the money must be collected. Like Joyce's boy peering into the darkened rafters of the Araby bazaar and lamenting the vanity of his impulsive act, Sammy says at the end of *his* story, "My stomach kind of fell as I felt how hard the world was going to be to me hereafter" (196).

Hereafter . . . it's an oddly formal word with which to conclude for Sammy, who is otherwise a most colloquial storyteller. Does Updike mean to hint that Sammy's epiphany bears intimations of immortality?—and not very positive ones at that? Joyce's boy would seem simply to have matured as a result of his insight, to have become better equipped for life as an adult.[6] Though convinced as a youth that his devotion to Mangan's sister was divinely driven, he has come to realize—as his older, more articulate narrative voice makes clear—that he had, back then, been "a creature driven and derided by vanity" (Joyce 35). Looking backward, Joyce's narrator has resolved his earlier confusion of spirit and libido, and can recount for us, however wistfully, how that resolution came about. Updike's Sammy, by comparison, speaks less retrospectively. He is still 19 at the end of his story, and still looking around for the girls in the parking lot, though "they're gone, of course" ("A&P" 196). Sammy looks ahead—into the life that lies before him, even perhaps (given that concluding word) at his own uncertain path to the Hereafter. And he sees nothing very clearly, only indefiniteness.

---

[6] I do not mean, in so saying, to ignore the great social, political and religious density of "Araby," which reverberates far beyond Updike's transformations of the story. That density is brilliantly explicated by Harry Stone in "'Araby' and the Writings of James Joyce."

Both protagonists have come to realize that romantic gestures—in fact, that the whole chivalric world view—are, in modern times, counterproductive. That there are, however, for American adolescents in post-atomic, Cold War New England, any viable alternatives is less assured. Sammy's is the more ambivalent epiphany.

WORKS CITED

Bunyan, John. *The Pilgrim's Progress.* London: Oxford UP, 1904.

Dessner, Lawrence Jay. "Irony and Innocence in John Updike's 'A&P.'" *Studies in Short Fiction* 25 (1988): 315–17.

Detweiler, Robert. *John Updike.* Rev. ed. Boston: Twayne, 1984.

Emmett, Paul J. "A Slip That Shows: Updike's 'A&P.'" *Notes on Contemporary Literature* 15.2 (1985): 9–11.

Gross, Marjorie Hill. "Widening Perceptions in Updike's 'A&P.'" *Notes on Contemporary Literature* 14.5 (1984): 8.

Hamilton, Alice and Kenneth. *The Elements of John Updike.* n.p.: William B. Eerdmans, 1970.

Joyce, James. *Dubliners* New York: Viking, 1958.

Mizener, Arthur. "Behind the Dazzle Is a Knowing Eye." Rev. of *Pigeon Feathers and Other Stories,* by John Updike. *New York Times Book Review* 18 March 1962: 1, 29.

Oates, Joyce Carol. Rev. of *The Coup,* by John Updike. *New Republic* 6 Jan. 1959: 32–35.

Overmyer, Janet. "Courtly Love in the A&P." *Notes on Contemporary Literature* 2 (1972): 5.

Porter, M. Gilbert. "John Updike's 'A&P'": The Establishment and an Emersonian Cashier." *English Journal* 61 (1972): 1156.

Schiff, James A. "Updike's *Scarlett Letter* Trilogy: Recasting an American Myth." *Studies in American Fiction* 20 (1992): 17–32.

Stone, Harry. "'Araby' and the Writings of James Joyce." *Antioch Review* 25 (1965) 375–410.

Strandberg, Victor. "John Updike and the Changing of the Gods." *Mosaic: A Journal for the Comparative Study of Literature and Ideas,* 12 (1978): 157–75.

Updike, John. "You'll Never Know, Dear, How Much I Love You." *Olinger Stories* New York: Vintage, 1964.

———. "A&P." *Pigeon Feathers and Other Stories.* New York: Knopf, 1962. 187–96.

———. "Questions Concerning Giacomo." *New Yorker* (6 Apr. 1968): 167–68, 171–74.

Yates, Norris W. "The Doubt and Faith of John Updike." *College English* 26 (1965) 469–74.

LAWRENCE JAY DESSNER

Irony and Innocence
in John Updike's "A & P"
Summer, 1988

John Updike's short story "A&P," first published in *The New Yorker*[1] and then in *Pigeon Feathers and Other Stories* (1962),[2] has become something of a classic of college literature anthologies,[3] and no doubt the story's brevity and its outrageously naive yet morally ambitious teen-age hero have much to do with that status.[4] Part of the story's appeal, too, derives from the fact that the wild comedy of its boisterously inventive and rebellious narrator modulates at its end into a gentle but benign sobriety. Moments after Sammy dramatically surrenders his job at the cash register to protest the unchivalrous treatment of the three girls in swim suits who have broken the store's unwritten dress code, we may rejoice in the condescending yet charming irony of his naive conclusion: "I felt how hard the world was going to be to me hereafter." Sammy surely overrates the harm he has done to his prospects.[5] We chuckle at his groundless apprehension and at Updike's momentarily convincing if mischievous pretense that the world is benign. We are gladdened to have had our disbelief suspended.

---

[1] 37 (July 22, 1961), 22–24.

[2] (New York: Knopf, 1962), pp. 187–96. I quote from this text, which varies only slightly from its serial form: the girl's "can" had been her "backside"; her chest, "like a dented sheet of metal tilted in the light," had been "hanging" rather than "tilted"; "Central Street" had been "the main street"; and the clothes Sammy did not have to collect before making his dramatic entrance from the store were his "coat and ear muffs," rather than "coat and galoshes." The revised version adds a dash at "(*splat*)!—the" (p. 194), "top of" to "drop the bow tie on . . . it," and a sentence which follows this addition: "The bow tie is theirs, if you've ever wondered" (p. 196).

[3] Ronald E. McFarland, "Updike and the Critics: Reflections on 'A&P,'" *Studies in Short Fiction,* 20 (1983), 95–96, documents this assertion.

[4] McFarland, pp. 97–99, credits the story's "ambiguity, its ironic doubleness" (p. 97) for its popularity.

[5] Janet Overmyer, "Courtly Love in the A&P," *Notes on Contemporary Literature,* 2 (1972), 5, suggests that Sammy's closing remark about his now-clouded future refers to his "loss of innocence" about the prospects of courtly love's "idealization of the beloved" in the real world.

But this analysis of the tonal satisfactions of the ending overlooks its deeper irony and the story's more considerable structural design on which that irony depends. The running theme which links the bulk of the story's incidents repeatedly demonstrates Sammy's inability to imagine himself personally at risk. The expectation this motif awakens in us is that Sammy will continue to underrate the world's dangers. At the story's end, however, he surprises us by *overrating* them—although with ludicrous and touching selectivity.

The first of these dangers to present itself to Sammy is either penury or a neurotic meanness of spirit. The middle-aged customer who gives Sammy "hell" for ringing up her box of crackers twice is in Sammy's quick calculation, "about fifty," and a "witch" of the sort he's learned once flourished in nearby Salem. He notices the "rouge on her cheekbones and no eyebrows" but nothing else that might stir him in the direction of sympathy. That the malicious intent he silently accuses her of, and the "sheep"-like behavior, "like scared pigs in a chute," of the other "houseslaves in pin curlers" who draw his sarcastic ire, might have sources in something other than the one's motiveless malignity and the others' dullness of character, does not occur to Sammy. He calls the "pigs" "scared" as if he himself had never known fear, as if no one ever had, as if "scared" were a term of opprobrium. He blames the customers of his A&P for being "houseslaves" without any sensitivity to the misfortunes of literal or metaphoric slavery the epithet points to. The thought that his mother, or his wife to be, might herself deserve something more generous than loathing for having "varicose veins [like those] mapping [the shoppers'] legs" does not break the shell of the boy's innocence.[6]

Nor does he know, or care about, the circumstances that might lead one—himself for instance—to a career as a laborer in the city's Department of Streets and Sewers. The men who have come to such employment are to him nothing more than "old freeloaders." Similarly, the "old party in baggy gray pants who stumbles up [to his checkout lane] with four giant cans of

---

[6] M. Gilbert Porter, "John Updike's 'A&P': The Establishment and an Emersonian Cashier," *English Journal* 61 (1972), 1156, states that Sammy's judgments on those he surveys from his checkout counter are "essentially true." "Many of them," he says, "have become [unlike Sammy] indifferent to beauty in any form." Sammy's response to Queenie is said to be "mainly . . . aesthetic," although McMahon's "interest is clearly erotic." Whatever Sammy's or Updike's relationship to the 1960's youth culture and its reckless self-glorification, Porter's loyalties seem clear. Marjorie Hill Gross, "Widening Perceptions in Updike's 'A&P'," *Notes on Contemporary Literature*, 14 (1984), 8, celebrates a Sammy who has "broken out of the . . . confining viewpoint of the sexist."

pineapple juice" evokes in Sammy nothing more than the thoroughly self-satisfied question, "what do these bums *do* with all the pineapple juice? I've often asked myself." There is no malice in that "bums," merely the guileless narcissism of youth. We laugh with Sammy more than we laugh at him. How grand it must be to know nothing at all about marginal employment or implacable constipation!

Sammy sneers at the store manager for "haggling with a truck full of cabbages"—and by extension sneers at all those who grow, transport, even eat, such mundane stuff. He is entranced and made enviously defensive by his notion that the underclad younger shoppers inhabit a higher social station than his own. His reflections on this topic permit him a kindly smirk not only at his own family's lower middle-class predilections but also at their better's sartorial usages. "Ice-cream coats" in his mocking name for their formal summer attire. Of his own eventual settling into or battling to gain or retain a standing in the social hierarchy, he is merrily unaware.

Sammy shamelessly ogles the three girls and reports on his sudden bodily weakness when one of them hands him a dollar bill taken from her bodice, but when McMahon, who works behind "the meat counter," follows them with his eyes while "patting his mouth" in the embarrassed simulation of yawning boredom, Sammy watches without an iota of masculine fellow feeling. McMahon *is* what Sammy doesn't realize he may someday consider himself fortunate to have become: McMahon is "old." To Sammy *his* ogling the girls is absurd, ludicrous, grotesque, even distasteful, a response Sammy neatly expresses when he says that McMahon, the butcher, is "sizing up their joints."

Sammy's tenure at the check-out counter at the A&P has exposed him to a fair sampling of the ordinary range of insult and indignity with which adults are forced to compromise. The fact that his observations, so marvelously acute and so precisely and delightfully expressed, have not led him to the slightest insight into his own membership in the family of the sons of Adam culminates in the surprising double irony of the story's conclusion. While enormously overrating the world's subsequent interest in his own employment history, Sammy enormously underrates the range and reach of the adult world's terrors, those necessities which do indeed lie in wait for him, the exhibition of which has comprised the essential bulk of his narrative.

Sammy renounces his allegiance to the A&P for their sake, but the girls are gone when he seeks them on the street; and when he looks back through the store's "big windows," he "could see Lengel," the offending store manager, standing in for him at the cash register. "His face was dark gray and his back stiff," says Sammy, "as if he'd just had an injection of iron. . . ." We know that Lengel had "been a friend of [Sammy's] parents for years" and that he had asked Sammy to reconsider quitting for their sakes. Surely the "dark gray" of his face is the sign of something other than the proud obstinacy Sammy believes it to be. But from the story's beginning to here at its very end, Sammy gets it wrong. The payoff of this theme ought to be Sammy's *lack* of concern for the consequences of his precipitous renunciation of his job. The irony turns in on itself when he doesn't even get *that* right. Our chuckles at his overestimation of the trials which await him are seasoned with a soupçon of kindly concern for him that has been prompted by his underestimation of all those ordeals of which his narrative has so forcefully and comically reminded us—but not him. Sammy, like the frightened child in Philip Levine's poem "To a Child Trapped in Barber Shop," thinks that his "life is over." The poem's narrator, like our story's, reminds his protagonist with wistful affection that "it's just begun."

RONALD E. MCFARLAND

Updike and the Critics:
Reflections on "A & P"
Spring–Summer 1983

During the twenty years since its appearance in *Pigeon Feathers* (1962), "A&P" has been established as John Updike's most widely read short story.[1] Its popularity among anthologists, as recourse to the listings in *Studies in Short Fiction* demonstrates, has made the story standard reading for thousands of college and high school students.[2] It has appeared in over twenty anthologies since its inclusion in Douglas and Sylvia Angus's *Contemporary American Short Stories* in 1967. What accounts for the continuing popularity of this particular story?

The reviewers greeted *Pigeon Feathers* with that peculiar damnation-by-hyperbolic-praise which continues to plague Updike. Arthur Mizener began his page-one review in *New York Times Book Review* by hailing Updike as

---

[1] The story first appeared in *New Yorker*, 22 July 1961, pp. 22–4. My text is *Pigeon Feathers* (New York: Knopf, 1962), 187–196. Quotations and allusions will be cited by page number in the essay.

[2] See in particular *Studies in Short Fiction*, 13 (Spring 1976), 270, in which compiler Landon C. Burns lists the story in ten anthologies. In his first compilation, *Studies in Short Fiction*, 7 (Winter 1970), Burns located the story in seven anthologies.

"the most talented writer of his age in America (he is 30 today) and perhaps the most serious," only to warn later of the dangers of Updike's Joycean "verbal brilliance" and of the sometimes awkward conflict in his work between "wit and insight."[3] He did not mention "A&P." J. M. Edelstein, who made a passing comment on "A&P" but focused on "Lifeguard," found Updike's work "rewarding," but also "terribly frustrating."[4] Along with the stories' "glitter and shine," occasional "dazzle," their "irony" and "neat felicity," Edelstein also detected "a cleverness and an obvious mannerism that becomes tiresome." Granville Hicks did not mention the story in his lead review for *Saturday Review*, though his praise of Updike ("bold, resourceful, and intensely serious") was more unstinting than that of other reviewers.[5] Only the unsigned reviewer for *Time*, who began, "John Updike is a brilliant writer who has so far failed to write a brilliant book,"[6] reflected upon "A&P." But here, too, the damning with exaggerated praise was evident. Lauding "A&P" as the best story in *Pigeon Feathers*, the reviewer concluded that "it is as forgettable as last week's *New Yorker*."

Regardless of this indifferent reception, "A&P" has emerged as Updike's best known story. One reason that anthologists have embraced the story is probably their awareness of audience. Sammy, the 19-year-old check out boy, has natural appeal to a classroom full of 18- and 19-year-olds. His colloquial usages make him "accessible" to college-age readers, and the frequently remarked similarities with J. D. Salinger's Holden Caulfield have probably added to his appeal.[7]

In his instructor's handbook, R. V. Cassill characterizes Sammy as "a goodnatured, average boy" with "a vague preference for beauty, liberty, youth, and recklessness as against the stultifying cant of a stodgy civilization."[8] This has been the main trend of the critical response to Sammy as a

---

[3]   Arthur Mizener, "Behind the Dazzle is a Knowing Eye," *New York Times Book Review*, 18 March 1962, p. 1.

[4]   J. M. Edelstein, "The Security of Memory," *New Republic*, 14 May 1962, p. 30.

[5]   Granville Hicks, "Mysteries of the Commonplace," *Saturday Review*, 17 March 1962, p. 21.

[6]   *Time*, 16 March 1962, p. 86.

[7]   The kinship with Holden Caulfield, from *The Catcher in the Rye* (1951), has been noted by M. Gilbert Porter in "John Updike's 'A&P': The Establishment and the Emersonian Cashier," *English Journal*, 61 (November 1972) and by Donald J. Greiner in *The Other John Updike* (Athens: Ohio University Press, 1981), p. 118.

[8]   R. V. Cassill, "Instructor's Handbook," *The Norton Anthology of Short Fiction*, (New York: Norton, 1977), pp. 202, 203.

character. "He will not always be understood," Rachael C. Burchard writes, "but he refuses to be captured by conformity and monotony."[9] Hailing "A&P" as "one of the brilliant pieces" in *Pigeon Feathers,* Robert Detweiler finds that with his act Sammy "achieves a new integrity, one that divorces him from his unthinking conservative environment."[10] The most effusive admiration of Sammy, however, is provided in M. Gilbert Porter's essay, which discovers Emersonian qualities of various sorts in the protagonist and which argues that the "histrionic" aspect of his gesture "does not detract from the basic nobility of his chivalric intent, nor does it reduce the magnitude of his personal commitment."[11] Sammy, Porter concludes, "has chosen to live honestly and meaningfully."[12] This decision, presumably, makes him an Emersonian character rather than an ordinary fellow who, one may surmise, elects to live dishonestly and meaninglessly. Porter admits that Sammy's view of the adult world is "harsh," but he also finds it "essentially true."[13]

An important reason for the continuing attractiveness of "A&P," however, as is often the case with stories which prove to be of interest to literary critics and other serious readers, is its ambiguity, or, more narrowly, the ironic doubleness with which the protagonist is presented. Caught up in the colloquial comedy of Sammy's narration, the reader tends to view the story (and especially the protagonist) uncritically, thus discovering in Sammy at least a Quixotic type of nobility. Shortly after it was published, William Peden described the story as "trivial rather than significant, and more dull than delightful,"[14] perhaps because he could detect little besides adolescent arrogance in the protagonist, though he did not elaborate. More recently, Donald J. Greiner, noting that the girls in the story, ironically, are not in need of Sammy's help, observes: "Sammy learns that no one welcomes or even tolerates idle idealism. Rather than insist on principle, he has merely shown off."[15] Suzanne Uphaus also detects the "ironic distance" between

---

[9] Rachael C. Burchard, *John Updike: Yea Sayings* (Carbondale: Southern Illinois University Press, 1971), p. 140.

[10] Robert Detweiler, *John Updike* (New York: Twayne, 1972), p. 68.

[11] M. Gilbert Porter, "John Updike's 'A&P': The Establishment and the Emersonian Cashier," *English Journal,* 61 (November 1972), 1157.

[12] Porter, p. 1158.

[13] Porter, p. 1156.

[14] William Peden, *The American Short Story* (Boston: Houghton Mifflin, 1964), p. 70.

[15] Donald J. Greiner, *The Other John Updike* (Athens: Ohio University Press, 1981), pp. 118–9.

what Sammy intends and what he accomplishes, "which reflects Updike's conviction . . . that the heroic gesture is often meaningless and usually arises from selfish rather than unselfish impulses."[16] Much of the impact of the story, as I shall demonstrate, derives from the ambiguity, the ironic doubleness, with which Updike has invested his protagonist.

In order to illustrate (in a couple senses of the word) this story, Updike creates what I will call "brand-name symbolism." From the HiHo crackers (p. 187) to the Falcon station wagon (p. 196), Updike's brand names are more than simply appropriate projections of the setting. They are symbols, comical, if only because of their nature and context, which have meaningful associations when properly considered. They also contribute to the ironic portraits offered throughout the story.

Sammy associates himself at the outset with HiHo crackers, and they are a fitting symbol for him—an ordinary, middle-class (not Ritz crackers) snack item. How seriously, then, ought one to take Sammy? How seriously does he take himself? The brand name connotes light-heartedness and high spirits. The movement of the story, and of Sammy's perspective, is from the easy gaiety and freedom of youth toward the "hard" realities of adult societal judgment. As Sammy observes, his parents think what has happened is "sad," but, although he sees that life hereafter will be hard for him, he doesn't yet see how unfortunate is his fall from boyhood.

The girl Sammy calls "Queenie" is associated with "Kingfish Fancy Herring Snacks in Pure Sour Cream: 49¢" (p. 192). (I recently priced a similar product at $1.98 for an 8-ounce jar.) The brand name not only fits the imperial Queenie, but also suggests the social class, the upper crust, to which she belongs. The incongruity of the common HiHo crackers and a luxury hors d'oeuvres like herring snacks anticipates one aspect of the hard lesson that Sammy will learn. Queenie's brand-name symbol represents a world completely alien to that of Sammy, who visualizes her parents and their stylish friends "picking up herring snacks on toothpicks off a big glass plate" (p. 193). As X. J. Kennedy observes in his instructor's manual, the unsophisticated Sammy "thinks martinis are garnished with mint."[17] The brand name that Sammy refers to as symbolic of his own family is Schlitz.

In the confrontation itself there are several ironies. The A&P, after all, is the subsuming brand name in the story. It is a democratic melting pot of sorts, a typically American institution where, just as the Atlantic and Pacific come together, so do crackers and herring snacks, and so do the proletarian

[16] Suzanne Uphaus, *John Updike* (New York: Frederick Ungar, 1980), pp. 125–6.

[17] X. J. Kennedy, "Instructor's Manual," *Literature*, 2nd ed. (Boston: Little Brown, 1979), p. 8.

(the "bum" in his baggy pants who buys pineapple juice), the bourgeois, and the patrician. All are equal, one might suppose, at the supermarket. Yet it is here that a standard of social decorum is asserted, so the irony cuts at the upper class girls. Sammy is no kinder to his reflections on the proletariat (including the streetworkers) and the bourgeoisie than Lengel, the manager, is in his treatment of the patricians. At the same time, the social code itself is undercut, for though it is distinctly bourgeois in nature, its aim is to sustain the appearance of "class" (the patrician). The code of decorum keeps the store from being what it would pretend to be. The supposedly elite upper class is, in fact, very casual, too casual, under the circumstances, for the snobbish middle-class manager.

Some less central brand-name symbols also figure in the story. McMahon, the butcher is mentioned in the context of Diet Delight peaches (p. 191), an ironic anti-product to that of his department. The only brand name (of a sort) associated with the town besides the A&P is the Congregational church, a standard, Protestant, middle-class denomination, which is virtually surrounded by such non-spiritual businesses as two banks, a newsstand, and three real estate offices. Finally, although the company is not named, record albums which denote a particular middle-class brand of music are alluded to: the Caribbean Six and Tony Martin Sings (p. 192). The common name of the popular singer contrasts with the presumably exotic sextet.

The ironic doubleness and ambiguity are most obvious, however, with the last brand-name symbol in the story, the "powder-blue Falcon station wagon" (p. 196). Associated with "some young married screaming with her children" and being a station wagon, the vehicle relates to the sheeplike customers, the women with varicose veins and six children (p. 191), and the fifty-year-old cash-register-watchers (p. 187). But the vehicle's model name, "Falcon," suggests predatory aggressiveness. Falconry is traditionally a sport of aristocrats, and poetically the falcon has been connected with the power of Christ (a sort of anti-type to the dove). The vehicle itself, therefore, is a sort of self-contradiction. It is small wonder that the confused Sammy anticipates a hard life ahead. The world which he is entering creates just such confusing, ambiguous symbols for itself.

Some readers, as I have indicated above, have asserted confident and even dogmatic reading of Sammy's character. He is commonly seen as "standing for" youth (naive, but "right"), beauty, sensitivity, nonconformity, individualism, honesty, and excitement. It appears that the story has been promoted largely by those who read the protagonist in that way. Like Holden Caulfield, then, the altruistic (even chivalric) Sammy learns a hard lesson about reality, the "sad wisdom of compromise," as Detweiler calls it.[18] But Sammy lacks several essentials of the worthy hero. For one thing, he has no perspective on his situation. He can judge the effects of his "gesture," apparently, only from a brief passage of time. Furthermore, despite what some readers have said, Sammy appears to have very little sensitivity, except, of course, to the obvious nubile beauty of Queenie and her friends (although they respond to it differently, both Stokesie and McMahon also perceive that beauty). Sammy's reaction to the angry customer early in the story and his lack of sympathy for the varicose-veined mothers simply indicate his immaturity and failure of compassion. His descriptions of customers as sheep, or as "scared pigs in a chute" (p. 195) may be funny, but a moment's reflection shows them to be simply jejune. Finally, by his own account, Sammy's "gesture" (the word is used advisedly, for it is a mere gesture) is intended to impress the girls who have, ironically, missed the whole show.

If my antithetical portrait of Sammy were the whole story, however, he would be no more engrossing as a protagonist than what I might call "Sammy the altruist," as portrayed by other readers. Sammy, in fact, achieves a certain degree of heroism not so much by his gesture, which initially appears to be selfishly motivated rather than a defense of principle, but by his insistence upon going through with it even after the girls have left. At the end, the reader perceives Sammy as both victor and victim. Against the many instances of his insensitivity and immaturity, the reader finds some signs at the end that Sammy is growing up. In short, it is only partly correct to say that Sammy is noble or chivalric, and it is only partly correct to say that he is acting on selfish impulses. Much of the continued popularity of the story derives from Updike's refusal to guide the reader to an easy solution.

At this writing, I can account for ten books or monographs published on the works of John Updike, a writer who, at fifty, may have his best work ahead of him. His facility with language and what David Thorburn describes as his "unmannerly fertility" may always be held against him.[19] The charges (particularly of his facile style) are reminiscent of those one encounters from time to time against F. Scott Fitzgerald. Robert E. Spiller wrote: "Fitzgerald's strength—and his weakness—lay in the sincerity of his

---

[18] Detweiler, p. 68.

[19] David Thorburn, "Introduction: 'Alive in a Place and Time,'" *John Updike: A Collection of Critical Essays,* David Thorburn and Howard Eiland, eds. (Englewood Cliffs, NJ: Prentice-Hall, 1979), p. 1.

confession and in the gift of words in which it was expressed."[20] Like Fitzgerald, Updike concentrates on a specific social milieu. Updike's subject, Thorburn writes, "is always some variation on the spiritual and communal enfeeblement of contemporary American society, particularly among the suburban middle class."[21] Like Fitzgerald's, Updike's reputation will have to wait a generation or two to be properly measured, but I think he will prove to be the major spokesman of a longer and more complex era (the 1960's through the 1980's) than the Jazz Age.

M. GILBERT PORTER

John Updike's "A & P": The
Establishment and an Emersonian Cashier
1972

> *Whoso would be a man must be a nonconformist.*
> *For nonconformity the world whips you with its displeasure.*
>
> (EMERSON, "SELF-RELIANCE")

"Right in the middle of town" surrounded by "two banks and the Congregational church and the newspaper store and three real-estate offices" stands Updike's symbolic A & P.[1] As supermarket, it is the institution where according to any newspaper advertisement, the *best values* in town can be found. It is the common denominator of middle-class suburbia, an appropriate symbol for the mass ethic of a consumer-conditioned society. And it is in this setting that Updike reveals, through what is almost a prose dramatic-monolog technique, the sensitive character of a nineteen-year-old grocery clerk named Sammy, who rejects the standards of the A & P and in so doing commits himself to that kind of individual freedom for which, as Emerson said, "the world whips you with its displeasure."

---

[20] Robert E. Spiller, *The Cycle of American Literature* (New York: New American Library, 1956), pp. 196–7.

[21] Thorburn, p. 4.

[1] John Updike, "A & P" from *Pigeon Feathers and Other Stories* (New York: Alfred A. Knopf, 1962). All subsequent page references are to this edition. The book is also available as a Fawcett-Crest paperback.

Like Fra Lippo Lippi and Holden Caulfield, Sammy tells his own story, and the crisis with which his story is concerned occurs on a quiet Thursday afternoon in Sammy's home town north of Boston. On a shopping errand, three teenaged girls in bathing suits come into the A&P which employs Sammy. At issue is the question of propriety: Does the attire of the girls satisfy the requirement of "decency" which the policy of the A&P demands? But because the manager is temporarily out of the store, the moment is not immediately forced to its crisis; and in the interim, as the girls wander through the aisles, Sammy reveals through his descriptions of the store and its customers that implicit set of values which will ultimately set him against community mores.

He has, first of all, an eye for quality. He speaks disdainfully, therefore, of such products in the store as "records at discount of the Caribbean Six or Tony Martin Sings or some such gunk you wonder they waste the wax on, . . . and plastic toys done up in cellophane that fall apart when a kid looks at them anyway" (p. 192). With its "fluorescent lights" and its "green-and-cream rubber-tile floor," and even the store itself presents to Sammy an artificial atmosphere, and he sometimes extrapolates from the A&P to the superficial home lives of its customers. Taking his cue from the Kingfish Fancy Herring Snacks, for example, Sammy imagines the parents of the attractive girls when they entertain: the men in "ice-cream coats" and the women "in sandals picking up herring snacks on toothpicks"; he compares his parents' parties, at which Schlitz is served in "tall glasses with 'They'll Do It Every Time' cartoons stencilled on." Prompted by his concern for what is meaningful, he implicitly rejects the pretensions of the one and the corniness of the other. But his discerning vision is focused most severely on the people around him in the store, on those who have, in Sammy's eyes, been dehumanized through long subjection to mindless routine.

Describing the unequivocal judgment of boys, Emerson said (again, in "Self-Reliance") that a boy, "looking out from his corner on such people and facts as pass by, . . . tries and sentences them on their merits, in the swift, summary way of boys, as good, bad, interesting, silly, eloquent, troublesome. He cumbers himself never about consequences, about interests: he gives an independent, genuine verdict." Such are the verdicts that Sammy hands down on the patrons of the A&P, rather harshly investing each with his most characteristic animal feature. The woman who catches him distractedly ringing up a box of HiHo crackers twice, for example, he calls a "witch," whose "feathers" he must smooth before she "snorts" and leaves. The customers in the aisles he sees as "sheep pushing their carts" or as "scared pigs in a chute." In examining the dulled nature of these patrons, he exclaims, "I bet you could set off dynamite in an A&P and the people would by and large keep reaching and checking oatmeal off their lists . . ." (p. 190). Sammy is repulsed by their insensitivity, their loss of individuality, and by the joyless, wooden nature of their existence.

And not only are they joyless and mechanical; they are ugly as well. Sammy feels he is surrounded by "houseslaves in pin curlers" and "women with six children and varicose veins mapping their legs" (p. 191). This is a harsh—though poetic—judgment, and some of his judgments are even un-fair (for example, when he calls the elderly man with the four cans of pine-apple juice an "old bum"), but the harshness, as Emerson noted, is mainly teenaged exaggerationese growing out of the typical tendency to make blan-ket judgments hastily and to place all individuals in their nearest category. Though harsh, his observations are essentially true. The housewives ap-parently do not take sufficient pride in their appearance; because of their slovenliness, they are more to be scorned than pitied. Whether it is their fault or not, the women with varicose veins are unlovely. Furthermore, many of them have become indifferent to beauty in any form. Though they live within short driving distance of the picturesque Cape Code coast, "there's people in this town," Sammy remarks disgustedly, "haven't seen the ocean for twenty years."

The presence, then, of the three bathing beauties is a refreshing change of scene for Sammy. To the graceless dowdiness of pin curlers and varicose veins, they offer the contrast of winsome innocence and supple youth. Though only one of the girls fully satisfies Sammy's rigid standards for qual-ity, the other two have something to recommend them over the common herd. One, for example, has "a sweet broad soft-looking can with those two crescents of white just under it . . ." and the other is, Sammy perceptively suggests, "the kind of girl other girls think is very 'striking' and 'attractive' but never quite makes it, as they very well know, which is why they like her so much . . ." (p. 188). The most attractive girl, whom Sammy dubs "Queenie," has "white prima-donna legs" and breasts like two smooth "scoops of vanilla." Sammy's response to this beauty is significant. About the expanse of flesh between her halter and her shoulders Sammy rhapsodizes: "It was more than pretty." And when she pays him with a dollar primly ex-tracted from "the hollow at the center of her nubbled pink top," he exclaims appreciatively, "Really, I thought that was so cute." Though certainly there is an element of physical attraction in Sammy's response to Queenie, mainly his appreciation is aesthetic. He celebrates her beauty, her youth, her poise. And Stokesie, his fellow-checker, joins him.

The attitude of McMahon, the butcher, toward the girls provides a dramatic contrast to Sammy's attitude. McMahon's interest is clearly erotic, not aesthetic. As the girls walk away from the butcher counter out of sight of the checkstand, all Sammy can see is "old McMahon patting his mouth and looking after them sizing up their joints." As a member of the older generation and as an officer of sorts in the hierarchy of the A&P, McMahon is clearly aligned with Lengel, the manager, whose attitude suggests a kind of John Endicott Puritanism.

According to Sammy, Lengel is "pretty dreary," but this capsuled evaluation is rendered even harsher by the implications of Sammy's metaphorical description of the manager: Lengel, Sammy reports, has been "haggling with a truck full of cabbages" (suggesting a fishwife) before he comes in and confronts the girls; it is his usual habit to "scuttle" (like a beetle) into the office behind the door "marked MANAGER," where he "hides all day" (like a rat) (pp. 192–3). As a close friend of Sammy's family, Lengel carries some parental authority; as a teacher in the Sunday school, he is a voice in the church; as the MANAGER of the A&P, he is a voice in the business community. In short, Lengel represents the Voice of The Establishment. As one of the "kingpins" who enforce "policy," he sees himself as the voice of authority, the guardian of the community ethic. Sammy even imagines Lengel "thinking all these years the A&P was a great big dune and he was the head lifeguard." In this role, then, and with his "sad Sunday-school-superintendent stare" (which equates flesh with sin), he delivers in the name of decency his pious judgment to the girls: "After this come in here with your shoulders covered. It's our policy" (p. 194). Asserting that they "*are* decent," Queenie leads her friends indignantly from the store.

Sammy, upon whom the issues underlying the incident have forced a decision, declares his intention to "quit." His gesture is both an affirmation of the girls' decency and a rejection of the A&P and the misplaced values for which it stands. That his act is a little histrionic results from his adolescence; it does not detract from the basic nobility of his chivalric intent, nor does it reduce the magnitude of his personal commitment. As Sammy prepares to leave, however, Lengel makes a final pitch for The Establishment. "You'll feel this," he warns, "for the rest of your life." But Sammy is not buying Lengel's line: He punches the "No Sale tab" and walks outside, where "the sunshine is skating around on the asphalt" (p. 196).

Sammy knows that Lengel's prediction is true. As he looks back into the store, he sees Lengel "checking the sheep through" and realizes that the world is going to be hard on him "hereafter." He is aware, of course, that he has separated himself from the flock, from the "A&P crowd," and has chosen to set himself against the majority—to incur that wrath which Emerson declared was the lot of the nonconformist. But Sammy has also realized that "once you begin a gesture it's fatal not to go through with it" (p. 196). He knows that in choosing to follow the dictates of his conscience he will often be at odds with the "kingpins" and policy-makers; but he knows a more important thing: That not to follow the voice of conscience is to be false to one's own integrity and therefore to live a lie, and Sammy has chosen to live honestly and meaningfully.[2] He intends to be a man. As he walks resolutely from the store, the Massachusetts air seems to reverberate with the approbation of its nineteenth-century tutelary spirit; and the reader recalls that sage's charged words from "Self-Reliance": "Your genuine action will explain itself, and will explain your other genuine actions. Your conformity explains nothing."

GEORGE STEINER

Supreme Fiction:
America Is in the Details
March, 1996

Since "Roger's Version," ten years ago, theology has become John Updike's "supreme fiction." That phrase belonged, famously, to Wallace Stevens. With time, vivid affinities are becoming evident between Stevens and Updike. They are the masters of a sensuous abstraction, profoundly American. In this new novel, "In the Beauty of the Lilies" (Knopf; $25.95)—scriptural, hymnic in its very title—Updike's immersion in the literature of American Protestant theology is awesome, as is the virtuosity of his pastiche:

> The young century was thronged with a parade of inventions that amused Clarence when little else did, and the presumptuous, ragged, hopeful sound of a doughty little motorrig brought a ray of innocent energy, such as messenger angels would ride to earth, into his invalid mood. The hoarse receding note drew his consciousness to a fine point, and while that point hung in his skull starlike he fell asleep upon the adamant bosom of the depleted universe.

---

[2]   I question, then, William Peden's rejection of what he calls "the deftly narrated nonsense of 'A&P' which concerns nothing more significant than a checking clerk's interest in three girls in bathing suits," *The American Short Story* (Boston: Houghton Mifflin, 1964), p. 70.

At the close of the novel, that sleep will turn into apocalyptic nightmare in the fire death, closely modelled on the Davidian cult disaster, of a sect in Colorado:

> Why does God set before us and Jesus this cup brimming with the wine of His wrath, with fire and brimstone and hailstones the size of a talent? Why not give us a nice Coca-Cola or cold cider? Jesus wanted it to pass. He was a young man, with a great future in preaching and healing. But He had to drink that cup, He had to be whipped and humiliated in His naked body and nailed to that cross by big ugly spikes right through the palms of His hands and hung there so He could hardly get breath into His lungs in order to take away old Adam's sin, the sin of the world.

After which flames and gas consume the Temple of True and Actual Faith: "Then there was no more pain, but for the briefest burning edge, like the crinkly orange margin that consumes the paper of a cigarette in advance of the growing tobacco ash."

Between that hot day in the spring of 1910 in Paterson, New Jersey, on which Clarence Wilmot, a Presbyterian clergyman, loses his belief in God and the crazed death of his great-grandson eighty years later, Updike deploys his panopticon. The magic is one of surrealism, but in a literal sense of the word. Things, objects, mechanical-industrial proceedings, interiors, the play of light on fabrics are detailed, anatomized, and held up for sensory inspection with a loving mastery that no other novelist at present can match. Catalogues of foodstuffs, house-hold goods, drugs, silent movies and talkies, engine parts take on a weird, suffocating life force, like rubber plants gone mad in a greenhouse. The real is made surreal.

When a young woman takes off her corset, she divides and parts herself "from the semi-elastic carapace, much as one splits the nubbled belly of a Maine lobster to get at the meat." In the textile mills, "hundreds of unravelling shuttles slapped back and forth in their wooden boats by the snapping levers, hundreds of harplike reeds beating in the weft, beating in, beating in, as the heddles lifted and lowered the alternating halves of the warp, lifted and lowered, twenty picks to the minute." We learn the penny prices of Olivilo Soap, Marrow's Boudoir Talc, Sodiphene, and Terra-Derma Laxative, and about the glossy magazines—*Liberty, Collier's, McClure's*—whose descent from "aspiring Manhattan towers" on a town like Basingstoke, Delaware, is verily an angelic visitation. When young Teddy, Clarence's feeble son, sickens at his first cigar, that nausea becomes lyric: "The end of the cigar was coming apart in his lips, and the cry of the spring peepers from the backyard pond that Horace Pruitt had dug and that was now sludging in sounded like a beam of sound itself swaying, surging, in waves." It is Norman Rockwell country, that of a miniaturist chronicler of the boundless texture of the everyday, incomparable in regard to sex, that "entertaining smooth chute into the dark-red bliss of things."

At moments, the acrobatics of precision, of language becoming the skin of perception, are such as to make it impossible to separate craft from parody. Here is Teddy's daughter Esther, soon after arriving in New York:

> At the Barbizon she found another hot-house, of young women in bloom; humid confidences and gushed news about men and clothes, waitressing jobs and *must* movies were shared from mouth to ear to mouth until it seemed the building had a single, female nervous system, vibrating each morning through the stacked floors to the same smell of coffee and the clanking of depleted shower pipes, flooding the halls with evening perfume as the girls swirled out on stiletto heels to their dates, *jeunes filles en fleur* menstruating on a single merged cycle and turning over in unison in the dead of night as they rose through the gauze of their dreams and sank back again.

The allusion to Proust is almost antithetical: the minutiae of description in Proust are translucid to symbolic significance, to mystery. In Updike, "the dark-red bliss of things" is just and fully that. The wonder is the surface. It is precisely here that technique and theology meld. In a world in which God is either dead or the object of homicidal lunacy, *things* have surged to fantastic, omnivorous life. The more blatant the fiction, the second- or third-handedness (Updike revels in simulating the non-world of movies, of photographs, of television), the more compelling the claim to real presence. The "depleted universe"—depleted by God's exit—has to be filled to brimming with stuff and artifice. The Good Book is the Sears, Roebuck mail-order catalogue. The "delivery"—probably the key word, with all its ambiguities—of a Popular Encyclopaedia, as broken Clarence hawks it from door to door; of the mail and the newspapers (Teddy becomes a mailman); of packaged sex and tinsel by Esther, the movie idol, reflects the appetite of the living, their panic before emptiness. Throughout, and with a dispassionate deliberation that Flaubert would have saluted, Updike favors the vegetable and the inanimate over the human. The foundation for the human was (a vanished) deity. Things can make it on their own.

Clarence, the lapsed man of the cloth, begets Teddy, who carries the mail and begets Esther, who changes her name, rises to glamour, and begets deranged Clark, whom the flames consume in expiation to a nonexistent but vengeful Moloch. Triste copulations alternate with even sadder fellations. History unfolds richly in the background. Currier & Ives will yield to CNN.

Distant World Wars, with Depression, the drama of a Lindbergh or a New Deal impinge, sometimes heavily, on the works and days of Paterson and Basingstoke. There is a new weekly, *The New Yorker*, whose cover "had a chalky drawing of white-faced shoppers walking at night . . . past a store window holding a Christmas tree and a hollow-eyed, sinister Santa Claus." The Eisenhower era coincides with the "triumphant, platinum-blonde phase" in Hollywood sex comedies and Esther's career. And the sixties turn out to be "a good decade for death," what with her mother, Ama (Teddy's wife), and J.F.K. As the saga ends, history and privacy fuse in a white heat: Teddy watches the incineration of his grandson on the national news. Between the clips "a commercial about a cruise ship that looks like a New Year's Eve party, with this big-mouthed woman singing how you should see her now."

John Updike's genius, his place beside Hawthorne and Nabokov have never been more assured, or chilling. One puts down this novel with the intimation that America is, very near its center, the saddest country on earth. As Updike puts it, repeatedly, "Have mercy."

Sample Student Research Paper

Tim Westmoreland

Professor Adkins

Literature 2101

5 April 1997

"A & P": A Class Act

John Updike's "A & P," like many of his works,
is a "profoundly American" story about social
inequality and an attempt to bridge the gap between social classes (Steiner 66). The story
is told from the perspective of an eighteen-
year-old boy who is working as a check-out clerk
in an A & P in a small New England town five
miles from the beach. The narrative is told in a
slangy, colloquial voice that captures a brief
but powerful encounter with a "beautiful but inaccessible girl" from another social and economic
level (Wells 46).

Sammy, the narrator, is working his cash register on a slow Thursday afternoon when, as he
says, "In walks these three girls in nothing but
bathing suits" ("A & P" 14). Lengel, the store's
manager--a Sunday school teacher and "self ap-
pointed moral policeman"--confronts the girls,
telling them that they should be decently dressed
(Wells 50). It is a moment of heightened embar-
rassment and insight for all parties concerned,
and in an apparently impulsive act, Sammy quits
his job. Although the plot is uncomplicated, what
is at the heart of this story is more complex:

Westmoreland 2

a noble gesture that serves as a futile attempt   Thesis
to cross social and economic boundaries that are   statement
all but unbridgeable.

Through Sammy's eyes we see the class conflict   Discussion of
that defines the story. The privileged young   class conflict
present in
girls in bathing suits are set in sharp contrast   story
to the few customers who are shopping in the
store. Sammy refers to the customers as "sheep"
and describes one of them as "a witch about fifty
with rouge on her cheekbones and no eyebrows"
("A & P" 14). Other customers are characterized
in equally mundane terms--for example, "houseslaves in pin curlers" ("A & P" 16) and "an old
party in baggy gray pants" ("A & P" 17).

Unlike the other customers, the leader
of the three girls is described as a "queen":
"She came down a little hard on her heels, as
if she didn't walk in her bare feet that much,
putting down her heels and then letting the
weight move along to her toes as if she was testing the floor with every step, putting a little
deliberate extra action into it" ("A & P" 15).
The mere fact that "Queenie" does not seem to
have walked barefoot much seems to hint at a
social gap between the girls and the other customers. However, it seems clear that Sammy realizes that Queenie and her friends come from
farther away than just the beach. They have come
to test the floors of the less well off and do it
openly, in defiance of social rules. In a sense,
they are "slumming."

Westmoreland 3

Queenie, whose name suggests her superior
status, clearly understands her position in social as well as sexual terms. She has come to the
A & P to purchase "Kingfish Fancy Herring Snacks
in Pure Sour Cream" for her parents, while Sammy
has to spend the summer working. Even the choice
of the exotic and expensive herring snacks hints
at their different backgrounds. Regardless, the
two act in ways that are not all that different.
Both are self-consciously trying out new roles,
with Sammy trying to rise above his station in
life and Queenie trying to move below hers. As
Queenie arrives at the register, Sammy observes,
"Now her hands are empty, not a ring or a bracelet, bare as God made them, and I wonder where
the money's coming from. Still with that prim
look she lifts a folded dollar bill out of the
hollow at the center of her nubbled pink top"
("A & P" 17). With this gesture, she not only
tests her own sexual powers but also sinks to
the level of the supermarket and its workers and
customers. Despite her act, though, Sammy knows
how different Queenie's world is from his:

> I slid down her voice into her living
> room. Her father and the other men were
> standing around in ice-cream coats and
> bow ties and women were in sandals pick-
> ing up herring snacks on toothpicks off
> a big glass plate and they were holding
> drinks the color of water with olives
> and sprigs of mint in them. When my

Analysis of Queenie's status and sexuality

Westmoreland 4

> parents have somebody over they get
> lemonade and if its a real racy affair
> Schlitz in tall glasses with "They'll
> Do It Every Time" cartoons stenciled on.
> ("A & P" 17)

As Updike says in a 1996 interview, "[Sammy] is a
blue-collar kid longing for a white-collar girl"
(Murray).

At this point in the story, as Sammy says,
"everybody's luck begins to run out" ("A & P"
17). Lengel, the store manager, (who, according
to Updike, was named after a strict boss for whom
his mother once worked) hints at "the cruel and
unethical" rules that govern matters of social
etiquette (Murray, Interview). In the story he
confronts the girls' breach of etiquette, telling
them that they are indecently dressed. " 'We are
decent,' Queenie says suddenly, her lower lip
pushing, getting sore now that she remembers her
place, a place from which the crowd that runs
the A & P must look pretty crummy. Fancy Herring
Snacks flashed in her very blue eyes" ("A & P"
18). Suddenly, Sammy can no longer be a detached
observer and, in a gesture of defiance, he quits.
The real question here is why he quits. Updike
himself muses, "I wonder to what extent his gesture of quitting has to do with the fact that she
is rich and he is poor?" (Murray, Interview).

Sammy confronts social inequality, but is
his response simply heroic posturing or an action
that expresses his longstanding frustration? In

Analysis of Lengal's treatment of Queenie

Analysis of Sammy's heroic gesture

Westmoreland 5

other words, does Sammy quit because of what Updike calls a "simple misunderstanding of how the
world is put together" (Murray, Interview) or
because he is "a boy who's tried to reach out
of his immediate environment towards something
bigger and better" (Updike, "Still Afraid" 55)?
Although his action may be the result of both--
Sammy even states it would be fatal not to go
through with his initial impulse--it seems likely
that he is taking a deliberate stand against what
he sees as social injustice. Unlike Queenie's
act, Sammy's gesture will have long-term consequences. As Updike points out, in Sammy's small
town everyone will find out what he has done,
and he may be "known . . . as a quitter" (Murray,
Interview). Sammy's understanding and acceptance
of these consequences ("'You'll feel this for
the rest of your life,' Lengel says, and I know
that's true"), and of the limitations his social class impose upon him, constitute his ini-
tiation into adulthood ("A & P" 19). Whether
quitting is Sammy's first step toward overcom-
ing these limitations or a romantic gesture he
will live to regret remains to be seen.[1] As Updike says, "How blind we are, as we awkwardly
push outward into the world!" (Updike, "Still
Afraid" 26).

Although it is true that both Queenie
and Sammy attempt to cross social boundaries,
the reasons for their actions are different.
Queenie's provocative gesture is well thought

Conclusion—
summarizes
major points
discussed in
essay

out; she deliberately relinquishes her trappings, her clothes and jewelry, and it is her position that allows her this privilege. She concedes, only for a few minutes, her dignity and wealth in order to flaunt her sexuality and her power. In contrast, Sammy chooses impulsively, in what Updike calls a "hot flash," a "moment of manly decisiveness," to take action and, ultimately, gives up both his dignity and his power (Murray, Interview). He gains only a brief moment of glory before he finds himself alone in the parking lot. In this instant, he confronts the social inequality and the unspeakable frustration it represents. According to Updike, Sammy cannot win, though in a "noble surrender of his position," he gains an understanding of the weight he must bear (Murray, Interview).

Westmoreland 7

Note

[1] In a recent E-mail message, Donald Murray agrees that Sammy's quitting will have implications for him that it will not have for Queenie and her friends. He goes on to say, however, that it is also possible that the young women will remain "imprisoned in their class," while Sammy may have a chance of escaping the limitations of his.

                                        Westmoreland 8
                        Works Cited
Murray, Donald. E-mail to author. 2 April 1996.
---. Interview with John Updike. Perkins 33.
Steiner, George. "Supreme Fiction: America Is in
     the Details." Perkins 66.
Perkins, Wendy, ed. The Harcourt Brace Casebook
     Series in Literature: "A & P." Fort Worth:
     Harcourt Brace, 1998.
Updike, John. "A & P." Perkins 14–19.
---. "Still Afraid of Being Caught." Perkins 24.
Wells, Walter. "John Updike's 'A & P': A Return
     Visit to Araby." Perkins 45.

Bibliography

This bibliography is selective. It does not include all articles written by Updike, only the ones most relevant to "A & P." Neither does the bibliography include secondary work on Updike's children's literature, essays, novels, play, poetry, or other short stories, unless that work includes significant commentary on Updike's general themes and style. For a comprehensive bibliography see B. A. Sokoloff and David E. Arnason, *John Updike: A Comprehensive Bibliography* (Norwood, Pa.: Norwood Editions, 1973) and Jack De Bellis, *John Updike: A Bibliography, 1967–1993* (Westport Conn.: Greenwood, 1994).

Works by John Updike

ARTICLES

Updike, John. "Green." *The New Yorker* 10 Sept. 1955: 31–32.

———. "Emergency." *The New Yorker* 24 Sept. 1955: 38–39.

———. "Building Decor." *The New Yorker* 1 Oct. 1955: 27–28.

———. "Adequate Wiring." *The New Yorker* 29 Oct. 1955: 23–24.

———. "Swifts and Stuffers." *The New Yorker* 17 Dec. 1955: 25–26.

———. "Rockefeller Center Ho!" *The New Yorker* 11 Feb. 1956: 26–27.

———. "Pre-Expulsion Yellow." *The New Yorker* 24 Mar. 1956: 20–23.

———. "Central Park." *The New Yorker* 31 Mar. 1956: 23.

———. "Our Own Baedeker." *The New Yorker* 31 Mar. 1956: 25–26.

———. "Voices in the Biltmore." *The New Yorker* 14 Apr. 1956: 32–33.

———. "Glance." *The New Yorker* 26 May 1956: 26–27.

———. "Outdoor Art." *The New Yorker* 23 June 1956: 19–20.

———. "Said Yonkers to Gloversville." *The New Yorker* 15 Sept. 1956: 36–37.

———. "Postal Complaints." *The New Yorker* 6 Oct. 1956: 33.

———. "Convincing." *The New Yorker* 10 Nov. 1956: 44.

———. "No Dodo." *The New Yorker* 26 Nov. 1956: 43–45.

———. "Bird Census." *The New Yorker* 5 Jan. 1957: 20–21.

————. "Resemblances." *The New Yorker* 2 Feb. 1957: 26.

————. "Green Grow the Yesses, O!" *The New Yorker* 23 Mar. 1957: 23–24.

————. "Old and Precious." *The New Yorker* 30 Mar. 1957: 26–27.

————. "Physiologist's Holiday." *The New Yorker* 20 Apr. 1957: 24–26.

————. "Spatial Remarks." *The New Yorker* 16 Nov. 1957: 41.

————. "Our Own Baedeker." *The New Yorker* 23 Nov. 1957: 43–45.

————. "Postal Complaints." *The New Yorker* 15 Mar. 1958: 31.

————. "Auction." *The New Yorker* 12 Apr. 1958: 36–37.

————. "Dinosaur Egg." *The New Yorker* 19 Apr. 1958: 31–32.

————. "Upright Carpentry." *The New Yorker* 10 May 1958: 29.

————. "Crush vs. Whip." *The New Yorker* 21 June 1958: 21.

————. "Metro Gate." *The New Yorker* 24 Jan. 1959: 28.

————. "The Assassination." *The New Yorker* 7 Dec. 1963: 45.

————. "The Assassination." *The New Yorker* 21 Dec. 1963: 21–22.

————. "An Arion Questionnaire: 'The Classics and the Man of Letters.'" *Arion* Wint. 1964: 5–100.

————. "Precise Language." *Commonweal* 22 Apr. 1966: 160–61.

————. "Beer Can." *The New Yorker* 18 Jan. 1964: 23.

————. "Modern Art." *The New Yorker* 11 Apr. 1964: 31–32.

————. "Eclipse." *The New Yorker* 2 Jan. 1965: 22–24.

————. "T. S. Eliot." *The New Yorker* 9 Jan. 1965: 26.

————. "Voznesensky Met." *The New Yorker* 26 Aug. 1967: 19–20.

————. "Letter from Anguilla." *The New Yorker* 22 June 1968: 70–80.

————. "Writers I Have Met." *The New York Times Book Review* 11 Aug. 1968: 2, 23.

————. "An American in London." *The Listener* 23 Jan. 1969: 97–99.

————. "Views." *The Listener* 12 June 1969: 817–18.

————. "Cemeteries." *Transatlantic Review* Sum. 1969: 5–10.

————. "The First Lunar Invitational." *The New Yorker* 27 Feb. 1971: 35–36.

————. "Dawn of the Possible Dream." *Sports Illustrated* 21 Feb. 1972: 38–45.

————. "Tarbox Police." *Esquire* Mar. 1972: 85–86.

————. "Three Texts from Early Ipswich: A Pageant." *Audience* Mar.–Apr. 1972.

————. "Why Robert Frost Should Receive the Nobel Prize." *Audience* Sum. 1972: 45–46.

————. "The Dilemma of Ipswich." *Ford Times* Autumn 1972: 8–15.

————. "Broad Spectrum of Writers Attacks Obscenity Ruling." *The New York Times* 21 Aug. 1973: 38.

————. "The Chaste Planet." *The New Yorker* 10 Nov. 1975: 43–44.

————. "Walt Whitman: Ego and Art." *The New York Review of Books* 9 Feb. 1978: 33–36.

————. "The Witch-Herbalist of the Remote Town." (book reviews) *The New Yorker* 23 Apr. 1984: 121.

————. "Twisted Apples." (Sherman Anderson's "Winesburg, Ohio") *Harper's Magazine* Mar. 1984: 95.

———. "T. S. Eliot: A Life." (book reviews) *The New Yorker* 25 Mar. 1985: 120.
———. "Howells as Anti-Novelist." *The New Yorker* 13 July 1987: 78.
———. "The Writer Lectures." *The New York Review of Books* 16 June 1988: 23.
———. "A Writer's Blocks." *Harper's* Jan. 1989: 36.
———. "The Sixties." *The New Yorker* 29 Nov. 1993: 159.
———. "Men's Bodies, Men's Selves." *Harper's* Nov. 1993: 17.
———. "Me and My Books: How Did They Assume a Life of Their Own?" *The New Yorker* 3 Feb. 1997: 38.

CHILDREN'S LITERATURE

Updike, John. *Bottom's Dream*. New York: Knopf, 1970. (adaptation of Shakespeare's *A Midsummer Night's Dream*)
———. *A Child's Calendar*. New York: Knopf, 1965.
———. *The Magic Flute*. New York: Knopf, 1962.
———. *The Ring*. New York: Knopf, 1964.

ESSAY COLLECTIONS

Updike, John. *Assorted Prose*. New York: Knopf, 1965.
———. *Golf Dreams*. New York: Knopf, 1996.
———. *Hugging the Shore*. New York: Knopf, 1983.
———. *Just Looking*. New York: Knopf, 1989.
———. *Odd Jobs*. New York: Knopf, 1991.
———. *Picked-Up Pieces*. New York: Knopf, 1975.
———. *Self-Consciousness: Memoirs*. New York: Knopf, 1989.

NOVELS

Updike, John. *Bech: A Book*. New York: Knopf, 1970.
———. *Bech Is Back*. New York: Knopf, 1982.
———. *Brazil*. New York: Knopf, 1994.
———. *The Centaur*. New York: Knopf, 1963.
———. *The Coup*. New York: Knopf, 1978.
———. *Couples*. New York: Knopf, 1968.
———. *In the Beauty of the Lilies*. New York: Knopf, 1996.
———. *Marry Me: A Romance*. New York: Knopf, 1977.
———. *Memories of the Ford Administration*. New York: Knopf, 1992.
———. *A Month of Sundays*. New York: Knopf, 1977.
———. *Of the Farm*. New York: Knopf, 1965.
———. *The Poorhouse Fair*. New York: Knopf, 1959.
———. *Rabbit at Rest*. New York: Knopf, 1990.
———. *Rabbit Is Rich*. New York: Knopf, 1981.
———. *Rabbit Redux*. New York: Knopf, 1971.

————. *Rabbit Run.* New York: Knopf, 1960.
————. *Roger's Version.* New York: Knopf, 1986.
————. *S.* New York: Knopf, 1988.
————. *The Witches of Eastwick.* New York: Knopf, 1984.

PLAY

Updike, John. *Buchanan Dying.* New York: Knopf, 1974.

POETRY COLLECTIONS

Updike, John. *The Carpentered Hen and Other Tame Creatures.* New York: Harper, 1958.
————. *Collected Poems: 1953–1993.* New York: Knopf, 1993.
————. *Facing Nature.* New York: Knopf, 1985.
————. *Midpoint and Other Poems.* New York: Knopf, 1969.
————. *Seventy Poems.* London: Penguin, 1972.
————. *Telephone Poles and Other Poems.* New York: Knopf, 1963.
————. *Tossing and Turning.* New York: Knopf, 1977.
————. *Verse.* Greenwich, Conn.: Fawcett, 1965.

SHORT STORY COLLECTIONS

Updike, John. *Afterlife and Other Stories.* New York: Knopf, 1994.
————. *Museums and Women.* New York: Knopf, 1972.
————. *The Music School.* New York: Knopf, 1966.
————. *Olinger Stories.* New York: Vintage, 1964.
————. *Pigeon Feathers and Other Stories.* London: Penguin, 1965.
————. *Problems and Other Stories.* New York: Knopf, 1979.
————. *Too Far to Go.* New York: Fawcett Crest, 1979.
————. *Trust Me.* New York: Knopf, 1987.
————. *The Same Door.* New York: Knopf, 1959.

Profiles

Brofman, John. "Inside Updike." *Life* 12 Mar. 1989: 10.
Ecenbarger, William. "Updike Is Home." *The Philadelphia Inquirer Magazine* 12 June 1983: 19–21, 24–25.
Hendrikson, Paul. "Updike Run: At 42, Still Making 'Em Look Easy." *National Observer* 1 Mar. 1975: 7.

Howard, Jane. "Can a Nice Novelist Finish First?" *Life* 4 Nov. 1966: 74–82.

"Perennial Promises Kept." *Time* 18 October 1982: 72–81.

"What Makes Rabbit Run? A Profile of John Updike." *People* 27 June 1983: 11.

Interviews

Pinsker, Sanford. "The Art of Fiction: A Conversation with John Updike." *The Sewanee Review* Sum. 1996: 423–33.

Plath, James, ed. *Conversations with John Updike.* Jackson: UP of Mississippi, 1994.

Reilly, Charlie. "Talking with John Updike." *Inquiry Magazine* 11 Dec. 1978: 14–17.

Biography

Greiner, Donald J. "John Updike." In *Dictionary of Literary Biography: American Novelists Since World War II.* Third Series. Eds. James R. Giles and Wanda H. Giles. Detroit: Gale Research, 1994. 250–76.

Samuels, Charles T. "John Updike." In *American Writers: A Collection of Literary Biographies.* IV. New York: Scribner's, 1974. 214–35.

Selby, Mabel M. Updike. *History of the John Updike Family.* Denver, Colo.: Sherry Redd-Kelly-Strobel, 1989.

Criticism and Commentary

Balbert, P. "Exuberances of Style in Pynchon and Updike: A Panoply of Metaphor." *Studies in the Novel* 15 (1983): 265–76.

Bloom, Harold, ed. *John Updike: Modern Critical Views.* New York: Chelsea House, 1987.

Bowman, Diane Kim. "Flying High: The American Icarus in Morrison, Roth and Updike." *Perspectives on Contemporary Literature* 8 (1982): 10–17.

Burchard, (Rachael) C. *John Updike: Yea Sayings.* Carbondale: Southern Illinois UP, 1971.

Carnes, Mark C. "Fictions and Fantasies of Early Twentieth-Century Manhood." *Reviews in American History* 24.3 (1996): 448–53.

Coale, Samuel C. "Marriage in Contemporary American Literature: The Mismatched Marriages of Manichean Minds." *Thought* 58 (1983): 111–20.

Detweiler, Robert C. *John Updike*. Rev. ed. New York: Twayne, 1984.

———. *Breaking the Fall: Religious Readings of Contemporary Fiction*. 2nd. ed. Louisville: Westminster John Knox, 1995.

Doody, Terence A. "Updike's Idea of Reification." *Contemporary Literature* 20 (1979): 204–20.

Eiland, H. "Updike's Womanly Man." *Centennial Review* 26 (1982): 312–23.

Finkelstein, Sidney. "The Anti-Hero of Updike, Bellow, and Malamud." *American Dialog* 7 (1972): 12–14.

Galloway, David. "The Absurd Man as Saint: The Novels of John Updike." *Modern Fiction Studies* 11 (1964): 111–27.

Gardner, John. *On Moral Fiction*. New York: Basic Books, 1978.

Gindin, James. "Megalotopia and the Wasp Backlash: The Fiction of Mailer and Updike." *Centennial Review* 15 (1971): 38–52.

Gingher, Robert. "Has John Updike Anything to Say?" *Modern Fiction Studies* 20 (1974): 97–105.

Greiner, Donald J. *Adultery in the American Novel: Updike, James, and Hawthorne*. Columbia: U of South Carolina P, 1985.

———. "Body and Soul: John Updike and *The Scarlet Letter.*" *Journal of Modern Literature* 15 (1989): 475–95.

———. *John Updike's Novels*. Athens: Ohio UP, 1984.

———. The Other *John Updike: Poems/Short Stories/Prose/Play*. Athens: Ohio UP, 1981.

Gullette, Margaret Morganroth. *Safe at Last in the Middle Years: The Invention of the Midlife Progress Novel*. Berkeley: U of California P, 1988.

Gratton, Margaret. "The Use of Rhythm in Three Novels by John Updike." *University of Portland Review* 21 (1969): 3–12.

Hamilton, Alice and Kenneth Hamilton. *The Elements of John Updike*. Grand Rapids, Mich.: Eerdmans, 1970.

———. "Mythic Dimensions in Updike's Fiction." *North Dakota Quarterly* 41.3 (1973): 54–66.

Hamilton, Alice. "Between Innocence and Experience: From Joyce to Updike." *Dalhousie Review* 49 (1969): 102–09.

Harper, H. M. *Desperate Faith: A Study of Bellow, Salinger, Mailer, Baldwin and Updike*. Chapel Hill: U of NC P, 1977.

Hendin, Josephine. *Vulnerable People: A View of American Fiction Since 1945*. New York: Oxford UP, 1978.

Hicks, Granville. "Generations of the Fifties: Malamud, Gold, and Updike." *The Creative Present: Notes on Contemporary American Fiction*. Eds. Nona Balakian and Charles Simmons. Garden City: Doubleday, 1963.

———. "John Updike." *Literary Horizons: A Quarter Century of American Fiction*. New York: New York UP, 1970: 107–33.

Hill, John S. "Quest for Belief: Theme in the Novels of John Updike." *Southern Humanities Review* 3 (1969): 166–75.

Hunt, George. *John Updike and the Three Great Secret Things: Sex, Religion, and Art.*
Grand Rapids: Eerdmans, 1980.
———. "Updike's Pilgrims in a World of Nothingness." *Thought* 53 (1978):
384–400.
Karl, Frederick R. *American Fictions 1940–1980.* New York: Harper, 1983.
Kazin, Alfred. "Professional Observers: Cozzens to Updike." *Bright Book of Life:
American Novelists and Storytellers from Hemingway to Mailer.* Boston: Little,
1973. 95–124.
Killinger, John. "The Death of God in American Literature." *Southern Humanities
Review* 2 (1968): 149–72.
Kunkel, Francis L. "John Updike: Between Heaven and Earth." *Passion and the
Passion: Sex and Religion in Modern Literature.* Philadelphia: Westminster P,
1975. 75–98.
La Course, Guerin. "The Innocence of John Updike." *Commonweal* 77 (1963):
512–14.
Luscher, Robert M. *John Updike: A Study of the Short Fiction.* Twayne Studies in
Short Fiction. 43. New York: Twayne, 1993.
Lyons, Eugene. "John Updike: The Beginning and the End." *Critique* 14 (1982):
44–59.
Macnaughton, William R., ed. *Critical Essays on John Updike.* Boston: G. K. Hall,
1982.
Markle, Joyce B. *Fighters and Lovers: Theme in the Novels of John Updike.* New York:
New York UP, 1973.
Mazurek, Raymond A. "'Bringing the Corners Forward': Ideology and Represen-
tation in Updike's *Rabbit* Trilogy." *Politics and the Muse: Studies in the Politics
of Recent American Literature.* Ed. Adam J. Sorkin. Bowling Green: Bowling
Green State U Popular P, 1989.
Miles, Donald. *The American Novel in the Twentieth Century.* New York: Barnes,
1978.
Miller, Miriam Youngerman. "A Land Too Ripe for Enigma: John Updike as Re-
gionalist." *Arizona Quarterly* 40 (1984): 197–218.
Morey, Ann-Janine. *Religion and Sexuality in American Literature.* Cambridge
Studies in American Literature and Culture. 57. Cambridge: Cambridge
UP, 1992.
Muradian, Thaddeus. "The World of Updike." *The English Journal* 54 (1965):
577–84.
Neary, John. *Something and Nothingness: The Fiction of John Updike and John Fowles.*
Carbondale: Southern Illinois UP, 1992.
Newman, Judie. *John Updike.* New York: St. Martin's, 1988.
Oates, Joyce Carol. "Updike's American Comedies." *Modern Fiction Studies* 21
(1975): 459–72.
O'Connell, Mary. *Updike and the Patriarchal Dilemma: Masculinity in the "Rabbit"
Novels.* Carbondale: Southern Illinois UP, 1996.
Olster, Stacey. "*Rabbit* Is Redundant: Updike's End of an American Epoch."

Neo-Realism in Contemporary American Fiction. Ed. Kristian Versluys. Post-modern Studies. 5. Amsterdam: Rodopi, 1992.

Pasewark, Kyle. "The Troubles with Harry: Freedom, America, and God in John Updike's *Rabbit* Novels." *Religion and American Culture: A Journal of Interpretation* 6.1 (1966): 1–33.

Patanjali, V. R. "John Updike's Fiction and His Themes." *The Literary Endeavour* 6 (1985): 114–19.

Peden, William. "Metropolis, Village, and Suburbia: The Short Fiction of Manners." *The American Short Story.* 2nd ed. Boston: Houghton, 1975. 30–68.

Petter, Henri. "John Updike's Metaphoric Novels." *English Studies* 50 (1969): 197–206.

Regan, Robert A. "Updike's Symbol of the Center." *Modern Fiction Studies* 20 (1974): 77–96.

Richardson, Jack. "Keeping up with Updike." *The New York Review of Books* 15 (22 Oct. 1970): 46–48.

Ristoff, Dilvo I. *Updike's America: The Presence of Contemporary American History in John Updike's Rabbit Trilogy.* New York: Peter Lang, 1988.

Robison, James C. "1969–1980: Experiment and Tradition." *The American Short Story, 1945–1980.* Ed. Gordon Weaver. Boston: Twayne, 1983. 77–110.

Rupp, Richard H. "John Updike: Style in Search of a Center." *Sewanee Review* 75 (1967): 693–709.

Samuels, Charles Thomas. "The Art of Fiction XLII: John Updike." *Paris Review* 45 (1968): 85–117.

———. *John Updike.* Minneapolis: U of Minnesota P, 1969.

Schopen, Bernard A. "Faith, Morality, and the Novels of John Updike." *Twentieth Century Literature* 24 (1978): 523–35.

Searles, George J. *The Fiction of Philip Roth and John Updike.* Carbondale: Southern Illinois UP, 1985.

Smith, Kent D. *Faith: Reflections on Experience, Theology, and Fiction.* Lanham, MD: UP of America, 1983.

Stafford, William T. "The Curious Greased Grace of John Updike, Some of his Critics, and the American Tradition." *Journal of Modern Literature II* (1972): 569–75.

Strandberg, Victor. "John Updike and the Changing of the Gods." *Mosaic* 12 (1978): 157–75.

Tallent, Elizabeth. *Married Men and Magic Tricks: John Updike's Erotic Heroes.* Berkeley: Creative Arts, 1982.

Tanner, Tony. *City of Words: American Fiction 1950–1970.* London: Jonathan Cape, 1971.

———. *Adultery in the Novel: Contract and Transgression.* Baltimore: Johns Hopkins UP, 1979.

Tate, M. Judith. "Of Rabbits and Centaurs." *Critic* 22 (1964): 44–47.

Taylor, Larry E. *Pastoral and Anti-Pastoral Patterns in John Updike's Fiction.* Carbondale: Southern Illinois UP, 1971.

Thorburn, David and Howard Eiland, eds. *John Updike: A Collection of Critical Essays.* Englewood Cliffs: Prentice-Hall, 1979.

Todd, Richard. "Updike and Barthelme: Disengagement." *Atlantic* 230 (1972): 126–32.

Uphaus, Suzanne Henning. *John Updike.* New York: Ungar, 1980.

Vargo, Edward P. *Rainstorms and Fire: Ritual in the Novels of John Updike.* Port Washington, NY: Kennikat, 1973.

Vaughan, Philip H. *John Updike's Images of America.* Reseda, CA: Mojave, 1981.

Verduin, Kathleen. "Fatherly Presences: John Updike's Place in a Protestant Tradition." *Critical Essays on John Updike.* Ed. William R. Macnaughton. Boston: Hall, 1982. 254–68.

Vinson, James and D. L. Kirkpatrick. *American Writers Since 1900.* Chicago: St. James P, 1980.

Wakeman, John ed. "John Updike." *World Authors 1950–1970.* New York: Wilson, 1975. 1464–67.

Walkiewicz, E. P. "1957–1968: Toward Diversity of Forms." *The American Short Story, 1945–1980.* Ed. Gordon Weaver. Boston: Twayne, 1983. 35–75.

Wood, Ralph. *The Comedy of Redemption: Christian Faith and Comic Vision in Four American Novelists.* South Bend, IN: U of Notre Dame P, 1988.

———. "Into the Void: Updike's Sloth and America's Religion." *The Christian Century* 24 April 1996: 452–57.

Wyatt, Bryant. "John Updike: The Psychological Novel in Search of Structure." *Twentieth Century Literature* 13 (1967): 89–96.

Yates, Norris W. "The Doubt and Faith of John Updike." *College English* 26 (1965): 469–74.

Zuckerman, Jerome, "Desperate Faith." *Studies in Short Fiction* 50 (1968): 387–88.

Zylstra, S. A. "John Updike and the Parabolic Nature of the World," *Soundings* 56 (1973): 323–27.

America at Mid-Century

Bailey, Beth L. *From Front Porch to Back Seat: Courtship in Twentieth-Century America.* Baltimore: Johns Hopkins UP, 1988.

Barker, Roger G. and Herbert F. Wright. *One Boy's Day: A Specific Record of Behavior.* New York: Harper, 1951.

Barone, Michael. *Our Country: The Shaping of America from Roosevelt to Reagan.* New York: Free Press, 1990.

Bowles, Chester. *American Politics in a Revolutionary World.* Cambridge: Harvard UP, 1956.

Branch, Taylor. *Parting the Waters: America in the King Years, 1954–1963.* New York: Simon & Schuster, 1988.

Breines, Winni. *Young, White, and Miserable: Growing Up Female in the Fifties.* Boston: Beacon, 1992.

Bremner, et al., eds. *Children and Youth in America: A Documentary History.* 3 vol. Cambridge: Harvard UP, 1970.

Brooks, John. *The Great Leap: The Past Twenty-Five Years in America.* New York: Harper, 1966.

Carter, Paul Allen. *Another Part of the Fifties.* New York: Columbia UP, 1983.

Denison, Edward F. *The Sources of Economic Growth in the United States and the Alternatives before Us.* New York: Committee for Economic Development, 1962.

Diggins, John Patrick. *The Proud Decades.* New York: Norton, 1988.

Dobson, John M. *A History of American Enterprise.* Englewood Cliffs: Prentice-Hall, 1988.

Dodds, John W. *Everyday Life in Twentieth Century America.* New York: Putnam, 1965.

Duden, Jane. *1950s.* New York: Villard Books, 1993.

Eisler, Benita. *Private Lives: Men and Women of the Fifties.* New York: Franklin Watts, 1986.

Ekich, Arthur Alphonse. *The Decline of American Liberalism.* New York: Longmans, Green, 1955.

Flanders, Ralph Edward. *The American Century.* Cambridge: Harvard UP, 1950.

Friedan, Betty. *The Feminine Mystique.* New York: Norton, 1963.

Friedman Milton and Rose Friedman. *Capitalism and Freedom.* Chicago: U of Chicago P, 1962.

Galbraith, John K. *A Life in Our Times.* Boston: Houghton, 1981.

———. *Economic Development.* Cambridge: Harvard UP, 1964.

———. *The New Industrial State.* Boston: Houghton, 1967.

Gilder, George. *The Spirit of Enterprise.* New York: Simon & Schuster, 1984.

Goist, Park Dixon. *From Main Street to State Street: Town, City and Community in America.* Port Washington, NY: Kennikat, 1977.

Halberstam, David. *The Fifties.* New York: Villard Books, 1993.

Harrison, Gordon A. *The Road to the Right: The Tradition and Hope of American Conservatism.* New York: Morrow, 1954.

Hart, Jeffrey Peter. *When the Going Was Good: American Life in the Fifties.* New York: Crown, 1982.

Hartz, Louis. *The Liberal Tradition in America.* New York: Harcourt, Brace & World, 1955.

Harvey, Brett. *The Fifties: A Woman's Oral History.* New York: HarperCollins, 1993.

Home, Quincy and Arthur Schlesinger. *Guide to Politics, 1954.* New York: Dial, 1954.

Irish, Marinn Doris. *The Politics of American Democracy.* Englewood Cliffs: Prentice-Hall, 1959.

Jackson, Kenneth T. *Crabgrass Frontier: The Suburbanization of America.* New York: Oxford UP, 1985.

Johnson, Paul. *Modern Times: From the Twenties to the Nineties.* Rev. ed. New York: HarperCollins, 1991.

Jones, Landon Y. *Great Expectations: America and the Baby Boom Generation.* New York: Coward, McCann, and Geoghegan, 1980.

Kaufmann, Carl. *Man Incorporate: The Individual and His Work in an Organized Society.* Garden City: Doubleday, 1967.

Kirk, Russell. *The Conservative Mind.* Chicago: Regnery, 1953.

Kowinski, William. *The Malling of America: An Inside Look at the Great Consumer Paradise.* New York: Morrow, 1985.

Layman, Richard, ed. *American Decades: 1950–1959.* Detroit: Gale Research, 1994.

Lewis, Peter. *The Fifties.* New York: Lippincott, 1978.

Low, David. *The Fearful Fifties: A History of the Decade.* New York: Simon & Schuster, 1960.

Lubell, Samuel. *Revolt of the Moderates.* New York: Harper, 1956.

Lukacs, John. *Outgrowing Democracy: A History of the United States in the Twentieth Century.* Garden City: Doubleday, 1984.

———. *Passing of the Modern Age.* New York: Harper & Row, 1970.

Manchester, William. *The Glory and the Dream: A Narrative History of America 1932–72.* Boston: Little Brown, 1974.

McCaffery, John K. M. ed. *The American Dream: A Half-Century View from "American Magazine."* Garden City: Doubleday, 1964.

McConnell, Gerald. *Thirty Years of Award Winners.* New York: Hastings House, 1981.

Merritt, Jeffrey. *Day by Day: The Fifties.* New York: Facts on File, 1979.

Miller, Douglas T. and Marion Nowak. *The Fifties: The Way We Really Were.* Garden City: Doubleday, 1977.

Milton, Joyce and Ronald Radosh. *The Rosenbergs: A Search for the Truth.* New York: Holt, 1983.

Montgomery, John. *The Fifties.* London: Allen, 1966.

Oakley, J. Ronald. *God's Country: America in the Fifties.* New York: Dembner, 1986.

Packard, Vance Oakley. *The Hidden Persuaders.* New York: McKay, 1957.

———. *The Status Seekers.* New York: McKay, 1959.

Rossiter, Clinton Lawrence. *Conservatism in America.* New York: Knopf, 1955.

Rothman, Ellen K. *Hands and Hearts: A History of Courtship in America.* New York: Basic, 1984.

Skolnik, Peter L. *Fads: America's Crazes, Fevers, and Fancies from the 1890s to the 1970s.* New York: Crowell, 1978.

Stevenson, Adlai E. *The New America.* New York: Harper, 1957.

Stone, I. F. *The Haunted Fifties, 1953–1963.* Boston: Little Brown, 1989.

Trager, James. *The People's Chronology.* New York: Holt, 1979.

Wakefield, Dan. *New York in the Fifties*. Boston: Houghton, 1992.

Whyte, William F. *The Organization Man*. New York: Simon & Schuster, 1956.

Wilson, Sloan. *The Man in the Gray Flannel Suit*. New York: Simon & Schuster, 1955.

Zinn, Howard. *A People's History of the United States*. New York: Harper, 1990.

———. *Postwar America: 1945–1991*. Indianapolis: Bobbs-Merrill, 1973.

Electronic and Media Sources

FILM AND VIDEO

The Music School. American Short Story Series. Videocassettes. Learning in Focus, 1976.

———. Chicago: Perspective Films. Videocassette.

Rabbit, Run. Dir. Jack Smight. Perf. James Caan, Jack Albertson, and Carrie Snodgrass. Warner, 1970.

The Roommates. Based on "The Christian Roommates," from *The Music School*. Dir. Nell Cox. Perf. Barry Miller and Lance Guest. American Playhouse. 1984.

Too Far To Go. Dir. Fielder Cook. Perf. Blythe Danner, Michael Moriarty, and Kathryn Walker. MTV, 1979. (Adapted for television on Mar. 12, 1979, as a two-hour dramatic special; later released as a commercial film.)

The Witches of Eastwick. Dir. George Miller. Perf. Jack Nicholson, Cher, Susan Sarandon, and Michelle Pfeiffer. Warner, 1987.

SOUND RECORDINGS

"More Stately Mansions." *The Esquire Collection of Great Fiction*. Audiocassettes. New York: Esquire Audio, 1985.

Of the Farm. Books on Tape.

"Poker Night." *The Contemporary Esquire Stories*. Vol. 1. Audiocassettes. Albuquerque: Newman Communications, 1986.

"Responding Records Sequence." Lexington: Ginn, 1973. Two sounds discs that include "We Only Came to Sleep," "Exposure," and "Thoughts While Driving Home."

S. Read by Kathryn Walker. Audiocassette. Audio Prose Library, Inc.

WORLD WIDE WEB SITES

Garner, Dwight. "The Salon Interview: John Updike." Salon. Online Posting. Internet. 16 July 1997. Available http://www.salon1999.com/08/features/updike.html.

Goldsmith, Judith. "A Biased Timeline of the Counter Culture." Online Posting. Internet. 16 July 1997. Available http://gopher.wel.sf.ca.us/11/Community/60sTimeline.

"John Updike." Online Posting. Internet. 16 July 1997. Available http://www.nytimes.com/books/97/04/06/lifetimes/updike.html.

"Lund's Office/Bookshelf/Thesis." Online Posting. Internet. 16 July 1997. Available http:/cal.bemidji.msus.edu/English/GA/lund/master/thesis.html.

Oates, Joyce Carol. "John Updike's American Comedies." Online Posting. Internet. 16 July 1997. Available http://storm.usfca.edu/~southerr/onupdike.html.

Tal, Kali. "The Sixties Project." Online Posting. Internet. 16 July 1997. Available http://jefferson.village.virginia.edu/sixties.

Yerkes, James. "The Centaurian: A Home Page for John Updike Info and Discussion." Online Posting. Internet. 16 July 1997. Available http://sss.users.fast.net/~joyerkes/index.html.

Appendix: Documenting Sources

A Guide to MLA
Documentation Style

Documentation is the acknowledgment of information from an outside source that you use in a paper. In general, you should give credit to your sources whenever you quote, paraphrase, summarize, or in any other way incorporate borrowed information or ideas into your work. Not to do so— on purpose or by accident—is to commit **plagiarism,** to appropriate the intellectual property of others. By following accepted conventions of documentation, you not only help avoid plagiarism, but also show your readers that you write with care and precision. In addition, you enable them to distinguish your ideas from those of your sources and, if they wish, to locate and consult the sources you cite.

Not all ideas from your sources need to be documented. You can assume that certain information—facts from encyclopedias, textbooks, newspapers, magazines, and dictionaries, or even from television and radio—is common knowledge. Even if the information is new to you, it need not be documented as long as it is found in several reference sources and as long as you do not use the exact wording of your source. Information that is in dispute or that is the original contribution of a particular person, however, *must* be documented. You need not, for example, document the fact that Arthur Miller's *Death of a Salesman* was first performed in 1949 or that it won a Pulitzer Prize for drama. (You could find this information in any current encyclopedia.) You would, however, have to document a critic's interpretation of a performance or a scholar's analysis of an early draft of the play, even if you do not use your source's exact words.

Students of literature use the documentation style recommended by the Modern Language Association of America (MLA), a professional organization of more than twenty-five thousand teachers and students of English and other languages. This method of documentation, the one that you should use any time you write a literature paper, has three components: *parenthetical references in the text, a list of works cited,* and *explanatory notes.*

Parenthetical References in the Text

MLA documentation uses references inserted in parentheses within the text that refer to an alphabetical list of works cited at the end of the paper. A typical **parenthetical reference** consists of the author's last name and a page number.

```
Gwendolyn Brooks uses the sonnet form to create
poems that have a wide social and aesthetic range
(Williams 972).
```

If you use more than one source by the same author, include a shortened title in the parenthetical reference. In the following entry, "Brooks's Way" is a shortened form of the complete title of the article "Gwendolyn Brooks's Way with the Sonnet."

```
Brooks not only knows Shakespeare, Spenser, and
Milton, but she also knows the full range of
African-American poetry (Williams, "Brooks's Way"
972).
```

If you mention the author's name or the title of the work in your paper, only a page reference is necessary.

```
According to Gladys Margaret Williams in "Gwendolyn
Brooks's Way with the Sonnet," Brooks combines a
sensitivity to poetic forms with a depth of emotion
appropriate for her subject matter (972-73).
```

Keep in mind that you use different punctuation for parenthetical references used with *paraphrases and summaries,* with *direct quotations run in with the text,* and with *quotations of more than four lines.*

Paraphrases and Summaries

Place the parenthetical reference after the last word of the sentence and before the final punctuation:

```
In her works Brooks combines the pessimism of Mod-
ernist poetry with the optimism of the Harlem Re-
naissance (Smith 978).
```

Direct quotations run in with the text

Place the parenthetical reference after the quotation marks and before the final punctuation:

> According to Gary Smith, Brooks's <u>A Street in</u> <u>Bronzeville</u> "conveys the primacy of suffering in the lives of poor Black women" (980).

> According to Gary Smith, the poems in <u>A Street in</u> <u>Bronzeville</u>, "served notice that Brooks had learned her craft . . ." (978).

> Along with Thompson we must ask, "Why did it take so long for critics to acknowledge that Gwendolyn Brooks is an important voice in twentieth-century American poetry?" (123)

Quotations set off from the text

Omit the quotation marks and place the parenthetical reference one space after the final punctuation.

> For Gary Smith, the identity of Brooks's African-American women is inextricably linked with their sense of race and poverty:
>> For Brooks, unlike the Renaissance poets, the victimization of poor Black women becomes not simply a minor chord but a predominant theme of <u>A Street in Bronzeville</u>. Few, if any, of her female characters are able to free themselves from a web of poverty that threatens to strangle their lives. (980)

[Quotations of more than four lines are indented ten spaces (or one inch) from the margin and are not enclosed within quotation marks. The first line of a single paragraph of quoted material is not indented further. If you quote two or more paragraphs, indent the first line of each paragraph three additional spaces (one-quarter inch).]

SAMPLE REFERENCES

The following formats are used for parenthetical references to various kinds of sources used in papers about literature. (Keep in mind that the parenthetical reference contains just enough information to enable readers to find the source in the list of works cited at the end of the paper.)

An entire work

August Wilson's play <u>Fences</u> treats many themes frequently expressed in modern drama.

[When citing an entire work, state the name of the author in your paper instead of in a parenthetical reference.]

A work by two or three authors

Myths cut across boundaries and cultural spheres and reappear in strikingly similar forms from country to country (Feldman and Richardson 124).

The effect of a work of literature depends on the audience's predispositions that derive from membership in various social groups (Hovland, Janis, and Kelley 87).

A work by more than three authors

Hawthorne's short stories frequently use a combination of allegorical and symbolic methods (Guerin et al. 91).

[The abbreviation *et al.* is Latin for "and others."]

A work in an anthology

In his essay "Flat and Round Characters" E. M. Forster distinguishes between one-dimensional characters and those that are well developed (Stevick 223-31).

[The parenthetical reference cites the anthology (edited by Stevick) that contains Forster's essay; full information about the anthology appears in the list of works cited.]

A work with volume and page numbers

> In 1961 one of Albee's plays, <u>The Zoo Story</u>, was
> finally performed in America (Eagleton 2:17).

An indirect source

> Wagner observed that myth and history stood before
> him "with opposing claims" (qtd. in Winkler 10).

[The abbreviation *qtd. in* (quoted in) indicates that the quoted material was not taken from the original source.]

A play or poem with numbered lines

> "Give thy thoughts no tongue," says Polonius,
> "Nor any unproportioned thought his act"
> (<u>Ham.</u> 1.3.59-60).

[The parentheses contain the act, scene, and line numbers, separated by periods. When included in parenthetical references, titles of the books of the Bible and well-known literary works are often abbreviated—*Gen.* for *Genesis* and *Ado* for *Much Ado about Nothing,* for example.]

> "I muse my life-long hate, and without flinch / I
> bear it nobly as I live my part," says Claude McKay
> in his bitterly ironic poem "The White City" (3-4).

[Notice that a slash [/] is used to separate lines of poetry run in with the text. The parenthetical reference cites the lines quoted.]

The List of Works Cited

Parenthetical references refer to a **list of works cited** that includes all the sources you refer to in your paper. (If your list includes all the works consulted, whether you cite them or not, use the title *Works Consulted.*) Begin the works cited list on a new page, continuing the page numbers of the paper. For example, if the text of the paper ends on page six, the works cited section will begin on page seven.

Center the title *Works Cited* one inch from the top of the page. Arrange entries alphabetically, according to the last name of each author (or the first word of the title if the author is unknown). Articles—*a, an,* and *the*—at the beginning of a title are not considered first words. Thus, *A Handbook of Critical Approaches to Literature* would be alphabetized under *H.* In order to conserve space, publishers' names are abbreviated—for example, *Harcourt* for Harcourt Brace College Publishers. Double-space the entire works cited list between and within entries. Begin typing each entry at the left margin, and indent subsequent lines five spaces or one-half inch. The entry itself generally has three divisions—author, title, and publishing information— separated by periods.*

A book by a single author

Kingston, Maxine Hong. <u>The Woman Warrior: Memoirs of a Girlhood among Ghosts</u>. New York: Knopf, 1976.

A book by two or three authors

Feldman, Burton, and Robert D. Richardson. <u>The Rise of Modern Mythology</u>. Bloomington: Indiana UP, 1972.

[Notice that only the *first* author's name is in reverse order.]

A book by more than three authors

Guerin, Wilfred, et al., eds. <u>A Handbook of Critical Approaches to Literature</u>. 3rd. ed. New York: Harper, 1992.

[Instead of using *et al.,* you may list all the authors' names in the order in which they appear on the title page.]

Two or more works by the same author

Novoa, Juan-Bruce. <u>Chicano Authors: Inquiry by Interview</u>, Austin: U of Texas P, 1980.

---

* The fourth edition of the *MLA Handbook for Writers of Research Papers* (1995) shows a single space after all end punctuation.

```
---. "Themes in Rudolfo Anaya's Work." Address
     given at New Mexico State University, Las
     Cruces. 11 Apr. 1987.
```

[List two or more works by the same author in alphabetical order by title. Include the author's full name in the first entry; use three unspaced hyphens followed by a period to take the place of the author's name in second and subsequent entries.]

An edited book

```
Oosthuizen, Ann, ed. Sometimes When It Rains: Writ-
     ings by South African Women. New York: Pandora,
     1987.
```

[Note that the abbreviation *ed.* stands for *editor.*]

A book with a volume number

```
Eagleton, T. Allston. A History of the New York
     Stage. Vol. 2. Englewood Cliffs: Prentice.
     1987.
```

[All three volumes have the same title.]

```
Durant, Will, and Ariel Durant. The Age of Napoleon:
     A History of European Civilization from 1789 to
     1815. New York: Simon, 1975.
```

[Each volume has a different title, so you may cite an individual book without referring to the other volumes.]

A short story, poem, or play in a collection of the author's work

```
Gordimer, Nadine. "Once upon a Time." "Jump" and
     Other Stories. New York: Farrar, 1991. 23-30.
```

A short story in an anthology

```
Salinas, Marta. "The Scholarship Jacket." Nosotros:
     Latina Literature Today. Ed. Maria del Carmen
```

LIST OF WORKS CITED

```
    Boza, Beverly Silva, and Carmen Valle. Bingham-
        ton: Bilingual, 1986. 68-70.
```

[The inclusive page numbers follow the year of publication. Note that here the abbreviation *Ed.* stands for *Edited by.*]

A poem in an anthology

```
Simmerman, Jim. "Child's Grave, Hale County, Ala-
    bama." The Pushcart Prize, X: Best of the Small
    Presses. Ed. Bill Henderson. New York: Penguin,
    1986. 198-99.
```

A play in an anthology

```
Hughes, Langston. Mother and Child. Black Drama An-
    thology. Ed. Woodie King and Ron Miller. New
    York: NAL, 1986.399-406.
```

An article in an anthology

```
Forster, E. M. "Flat and Round Characters." The The-
    ory of the Novel. Ed. Philip Stevick. New York:
    Free, 1980. 223-31.
```

More than one selection from the same anthology

If you are using more than one selection from an anthology, cite the anthology in one entry. In addition, list each individual selection separately, including the author and title of the selection, the anthology editor's last name, and the inclusive page numbers.

```
Kirszner, Laurie G., and Stephen R. Mandell, eds.
    Literature: Reading, Reacting, Writing. 3rd ed.
    Fort Worth: Harcourt, 1997.
Rich, Adrienne. "Diving into the Wreck." Kirszner
    and Mandell 874-76.
```

A translation

```
Carpentier, Alejo. Reasons of State. Trans. Francis
    Partridge. New York: Norton, 1976.
```

An article in a journal with continuous pagination in each issue

```
LeGuin, Ursula K. "American Science Fiction and the
     Other." Science Fiction Studies 2 (1975):
     208-10.
```

An article with separate pagination in each issue

```
Grossman, Robert. "The Grotesque in Faulkner's
     'A Rose for Emily.'" Mosaic 20.3 (1987): 40-55.
```

[20.3 signifies volume 20, issue 3.]

An article in a magazine

```
Milosz, Czeslaw. "A Lecture." New Yorker 22 June
     1992: 32.
"Solzhenitsyn: An Artist Becomes an Exile." Time
     25 Feb. 1974: 34+.
```

[34+ indicates that the article appears on pages that are not consecutive; in this case the article begins on page 34 and then continues on page 37. An article with no listed author is entered by title on the works cited list.]

An article in a daily newspaper

```
Oates, Joyce Carol. "When Characters from the Page
     Are Made Flesh on the Screen." New York Times
     23 Mar. 1986, late ed.: C1+.
```

[C1+ indicates that the article begins on page 1 of Section C and continues on a subsequent page.]

An article in a reference book

```
"Dance Theatre of Harlem." The New Encyclopaedia
     Britannica: Micropaedia. 15th ed. 1987.
```

[You do not need to include publication information for well-known reference books.]

```
Grimstead, David. "Fuller, Margaret Sarah." Encyclo-
     pedia of American Biography. Ed. John A. Gar-
     raty. New York: Harper, 1974.
```

[You must include publication information when citing reference books that are not well known.]

A CD-ROM: Entry with a print version

> Zurbach, Kate. "The Linguistic Roots of Three
> Terms." <u>Linguistic Quarterly</u> 37 (1994): 12-47.
> <u>Infotrac: Magazine Index Plus</u>. CD-ROM. Informa-
> tion Access. Jan. 1996.

[When you cite information with a print version from a CD-ROM, include the publication information, the underlined title of the database (<u>Infotrac: Magazine Index Plus</u>), the publication medium (CD-ROM), the name of the company that produced the CD-ROM (Information Access), and the electronic publication date.]

A CD-ROM: Entry with no print version

> "Surrealism." <u>Encarta 1996</u>. CD-ROM. Redmond: Micro-
> soft, 1996.

[If you are citing a part of a work, include the title in quotation marks.]

> <u>A Music Lover's Multimedia Guide to Beethoven's 5th</u>.
> CD-ROM. Spring Valley: Interactive, 1993.

[If you are citing an entire work, include the underlined title.]

An online source: Entry with a print version

> Dekoven, Marianne. "Utopias Limited: Post-sixties
> and Postmodern American Fiction." <u>Modern Fic-
> tion Studies</u> 41.1 (Spring 1995): 121-34.
> 17 Mar. 1996 <http://muse.jhu.edu/journals/
> MFS/v041/41.1 dekoven.html>.

[When you cite information with a print version from an online source, include the publication information for the printed source, the number of pages or the number of paragraphs (if available), and the date of access. Include the electronic address, or URL, in angle brackets. Information from a commercial computer service—America Online, Prodigy, and CompuServ, for example—will not have an electronic address.]

> O'Hara, Sandra. "Reexamining the Canon." <u>Time</u> 13 May
> 1994: 27. America Online. 22 Aug. 1994.

An online source: Entry with no print version

> "Romanticism." <u>Academic American Encyclopedia</u>. Sept.
> 1996. Prodigy. 6 Nov. 1995.

[This entry shows that the material was accessed on November 6, 1996.]

An online source: Public Posting

> Peters, Olaf. "Studying English through German."
> Online posting. 29 Feb. 1996. Foreign Language
> Forum, Multi Language Section. CompuServe.
> 15 Mar. 1996.
> Gilford, Mary. "Dog Heroes in Children's Litera-
> ture." 4 Oct. 1996. Newsgroup alt.animals.dogs.
> America Online. 23 Mar. 1996.

[**WARNING:** Using information from online forums and newsgroups is risky. Contributors are not necessarily experts, and frequently they are incorrect and misinformed. Unless you can be certain that the information you are receiving from these sources is reliable, do not use it in your papers.]

An online source: Electronic Text

> Twain, Mark. <u>The Adventures of Huckleberry Finn</u>.
> From <u>The Writing of Mark Twain</u>. Vol. 13.
> New York: Harper, 1970. <u>Wiretap.spies</u>.
> 13 Jan. 1996 <http.//www.sci.dixie.edu/
> DixieCollege/Ebooks/huckfin.html>.

[This electronic text was originally published by Harper. The name of the repository for the electronic edition is Wiretap.spies. (underlined)]

An online source: E-Mail

> Adkins, Camille. E-Mail to the author. 8 June 1995.

An interview

Brooks, Gwendolyn. "Interviews." <u>Triquarterly</u> 60
    (1984): 405-10.

A lecture or address

Novoa, Juan-Bruce. "Themes in Rudolfo Anaya's Work."
    New Mexico State University, Las Cruces,
    11 Apr. 1987.

A film or videocassette

"<u>A Worn Path</u>." By Eudora Welty. Dir. John Reid and
    Claudia Velasco. Perf. Cora Lee Day and Con-
    chita Ferrell. Videocassette. Harcourt, 1994.

[In addition to the title, the director, and the year, include other pertinent information such as the principal performers.]

Explanatory Notes

Explanatory notes, indicated by a superscript (a raised number) in the text, may be used to cite several sources at once or to provide commentary or explanations that do not fit smoothly into your paper. The full text of these notes appears on the first numbered page following the last page of the paper. (If your paper has no explanatory notes, the works cited page follows the last page of the paper.) Like works cited entries, explanatory notes are double-spaced within and between entries. However, the first line of each explanatory note is indented five spaces (or one-half inch), with subsequent lines flush with the left-hand margin.

TO CITE SEVERAL SOURCES

In the paper

Surprising as it may seem, there have been many
attempts to define literature.[1]

In the note

> [1] For an overview of critical opinion, see Arnold
> 72; Eagleton 1–2; Howe 43–44; and Abrams 232–34.

TO PROVIDE EXPLANATIONS

In the paper

> In recent years gothic novels have achieved
> great popularity.[3]

In the note

> [3] Gothic novels, works written in imitation of
> medieval romances, originally relied on supernatural
> occurrences. They flourished in the late eighteenth
> and early nineteenth centuries.

Credits

Jay Lawrence Dessner, "Irony and Innocence in John Updike's 'A & P'" by Jay Lawrence Dessner from *Studies in Short Fiction* 25 (1988): 315–17. Copyright © 1988 by Newberry College. Reprinted by permission.

Robert M. Luscher, Excerpted with permission of Twayne Publishers, an imprint of Simon & Schuster Macmillan, from *John Updike: A Study of the Short Fiction* by John M. Luscher. Copyright © 1993 by Twayne Publishers.

Ronald E. McFarland, "Updike and the Critics: Reflections on 'A & P'" by Ronald E. McFarland from *Studies in Short Fiction* 20 (1983): 95–100. Copyright © 1983 by Newberry College. Reprinted by permission.

Arthur Mizener, "Behind the Dazzle Is a Knowing Eye" by Arthur Mizener from *The New York Times,* March 18, 1962. Copyright © 1962 by The New York Times Company. Reprinted by permission.

Donald Murray, Donald Murray E-mail to Tim Westmoreland regarding "A & P." Reprinted by permission.

"Amid Onions and Oranges, a Boy Becomes a Man" by Donald Murray as appeared in *The Boston Globe,* April 9, 1996. Reprinted by permission.

Gilbert Porter, "John Updike's 'A & P': The Establishment and Emersonian Cashier" by M. Gilbert Porter. Copyright © 1972 by the National Council of Teachers of English. Reprinted with permission.

George Steiner, "Supreme Fiction: America Is in the Details" by George Steiner. Copyright © 1996 by George Steiner. Reprinted by permission of George Borchardt, Inc. for the author.

John Updike, "Still Afraid of Being Caught" by John Updike as appeared in *The New York Times,* October 8, 1995. Copyright © John Updike. Reprinted by permission.

"Lifeguard" from *Pigeon Feathers and Other Stories* by John Updike. Copyright © 1962 by John Updike. Reprinted by permission of Alfred A. Knopf, Inc.

"A & P" from *Pigeon Feathers and Other Stories* by John Updike. Copyright © 1962 by John Updike. Reprinted by permission of Alfred A. Knopf, Inc. Originally appeared in "The New Yorker."

Walter Wells, "John Updike's 'A & P': A Return Visit to Araby" by Walter Wells from *Studies in Short Fiction* 20 (1993): 127–33. Copyright © 1993 by Newberry College. Reprinted by permission.